COLLIDERS

When the barriers of reality crumble, a desperate alliance battles to save a world unmoored by ancient powers

---

By

Steve Foley

ISBN: 979-8-3302-8902-8

Dedication

To those who dare to push the boundaries of the known world and to the dreamers who envision what lies beyond the veil.

This book is for you.

Acknowledgment

Writing *Colliders* has been a journey as complex and exhilarating as the story itself, and I could not have completed it without the support and encouragement of many individuals.

First and foremost, I would like to thank my friends & family for their unwavering belief in my vision and for giving me the time and space to immerse myself in the creation of this novel.

I am deeply grateful to my friends and colleagues, especially those who provided feedback on early drafts, offering their invaluable insights and pushing me to refine the narrative until it reached its full potential.

A special thank you to the scientific community, whose research and discoveries in the fields of quantum physics and cosmology served as the foundation for the world of *Colliders*. Your work continues to inspire and challenge our understanding of the universe.

To my editor, whose keen eye and dedication helped shape this manuscript into the story it was meant to be—thank you for your tireless efforts and for believing in this project from the very beginning.

Finally, to the readers, thank you for joining me on this journey through the unknown. Your curiosity and imagination make stories like *Colliders* possible.

About the Author

Steve Foley is a multifaceted filmmaker, writer, and producer whose passion for storytelling spans across genres. He is the author of *Droplets for the Soul,* a novel that seamlessly blends spiritual insights with contemporary narratives, and the creator of numerous graphic novels that delve into the rich intersection of science fiction, fantasy, and reality.

With a strong background in digital project management and a keen interest in cutting-edge technological advancements, Steve's work often explores the intricacies of the human experience within a rapidly evolving world. His writing style, best described as that of a research scientist, combines meticulous detail with a profound understanding of the human psyche, offering readers a unique and immersive experience.

Beyond his literary endeavors, Steve produces House Music under the moniker DJ Chilly-T and leads The Fantasmagorium, a YouTube channel and podcast dedicated to pop culture and movie news. Currently, he is immersed in a variety of projects, including outlines for over 20 graphic novels and a highly anticipated sequel to *Colliders,* continuing the exploration of the delicate boundaries between worlds and the epic clash of science and mysticism.

Preface

Colliders began as an exploration of the unknown—the uncharted territories where science meets the mystical, and the boundaries of reality blur into the surreal. As I delved into the world of quantum physics and ancient mythology, I became fascinated by the idea that our pursuit of knowledge could lead us to places far beyond our comprehension, where the very fabric of reality is at stake.

This novel is not just a tale of adventure and discovery; it's a reflection on the human condition—our insatiable thirst for knowledge, our desire to push the boundaries of what is possible, and the consequences that come with it. As you journey through the pages of *Colliders*, I invite you to consider the delicate balance between ambition and hubris, science and faith, and the profound impact our actions can have on the world around us.

I hope *Colliders* will inspire you to question the nature of reality, explore the unknown with both curiosity and caution and embrace the infinite possibilities that lie at the intersection of science and mysticism.

Table of Contents

Chapter 1: The Anomaly 1

Chapter 2: Echoes of the Past...28

Chapter 3: The Gathering 60

Chapter 4: Crossing the Thresholds 96

Chapter 5: Cult of the New Dawn 128

Chapter 6: Fractures 164

Chapter 7: Convergence...202

Chapter 8: Call of the Horizon...235

Epilogue 267

Chapter 1: The Anomaly

The air in the cavernous chamber hummed with a low, thrumming energy. Fluorescent lights cast the concrete walls in a sterile sheen, unable to pierce the shadows that clung stubbornly to the massive circular machine that dominated the space. This wasn't your typical research lab. Beneath the sprawling government experimental base, nestled in the shadow of the Large Hadron Collider itself, a different kind of science was unfolding here. A forbidden kind.

Dr. Evelyn Shaw, her dark, tightly coiled hair, now streaked with silver pulled back in a tight bun, wove through the maze of cables and cooling ducts like a seasoned navigator. Her brow furrowed beneath the harsh light as she approached the heart of the beast – a colossal ring of superconducting magnets pulsating with an ethereal blue glow. This was it: *Project Exodia*, her brainchild, her obsession.

Exodia wasn't your run-of-the-mill particle accelerator. Its purpose wasn't to smash subatomic particles at ever-increasing energies but to breach the very fabric of reality itself. It was a desperate gamble, fueled by a cocktail of scientific ambition and a personal hunger that gnawed at Evelyn's soul. Ten years ago, a freak accident during a routine LHC experiment had taken her husband, a brilliant physicist himself. Exodia, in its twisted way, was a monument to him, a desperate attempt to reach across the veil and somehow bring him back.

A young technician, barely out of grad school, hovered around a console, his face pale in the flickering display light.

"Readings s- stable, Dr. Shaw," he stammered, his voice betraying his nervous energy. "Energy levels approaching critical peak."

Evelyn gave him a curt nod, her gaze locked on the ever-fluctuating lines on the monitor. Years of sleepless nights of endless calculations and simulations culminated in this moment. Today, she would either achieve a scientific breakthrough of unimaginable proportions or condemn them all to a fate worse than oblivion.

Taking a deep breath, she activated the final sequence. The air crackled as energy surged through the superconducting ring. The blue glow intensified, then pulsed violently, morphing into a blinding white light. The ground trembled beneath her feet. A high-pitched whine filled the chamber, building to a deafening crescendo that threatened to burst her eardrums.

Then, silence. An unnatural, oppressive silence that hung heavy in the air.

Evelyn stared at the ring, her heart hammering against her ribs. Had it worked? Had she opened a gateway to the unknown? Or had she unleashed something far more sinister? Slowly, tentatively, she reached out and touched a control panel. A single red light flickered on the console, a solitary symbol in a sea of darkness. It was a start. A terrifying, exhilarating start.

Panic flickered across the faces of her colleagues; their once-confident expressions were replaced by raw fear. But Evelyn, ever the pragmatist, knew fear wouldn't solve this. She slammed her fist on the control panel, the metallic clang echoing through the tense room.

"Shut it down! Initiate emergency shutdown sequence!" Her voice, usually laced with quiet authority, now held a desperate edge.

The air crackled with nervous energy as technicians scrambled to obey. Alarms blared, red lights strobed, but the anomaly on the monitor remained, a defiant gash in the cosmos. The shutdown sequence, designed for equipment failure, seemed powerless against this otherworldly intrusion.

Evelyn watched in horror as a tendril of inky darkness reached out from the anomaly, writhing like a living serpent. It pulsed with an unnatural light, casting grotesque shadows on the control room walls. A wave of nausea washed over her, laced with a primal terror that transcended any scientific explanation. This wasn't just a scientific anomaly; it felt like a malevolent presence, a cosmic entity reaching through the tear with a hunger that chilled her to the bone.

Then, a guttural shriek pierced the air, a sound that seemed to claw at the very edges of sanity. It originated from the anomaly, a harbinger of something monstrous clawing its way into their reality. She knew then that shutting down the LHC wouldn't be enough.

Yet, she dared to hope.

* * *

Marcus Flynn sat in his chair, the swivel back and forth like a pendulum ticking away the seconds of his downfall. His office was a study in contrasts - the plush leather of his chair clashing with the bare walls, the silver frames holding memories now too painful to stare at.

In the stillness, a muted news broadcast played on the computer screen, his own face flashing across the screen accompanied by words like "disgraced journalist" and "tampering with evidence."

He took a drag of his cigarette, the smoke curling in a cloud of regret and self-loathing. Turning away from the screen, his gaze landed on the photo frame. The image of his wife was a painful reminder of all he had lost - her love, her trust, her respect. He reached out, his fingers trembling slightly, and turned the frame face down, hiding her from view. He closed his eyes, leaning back into the chair.

Why, Markie? Why'd ya do it, love?

It had been a few months, and her words, along with the memory of her tear-stained, frustrated face, still haunted his thoughts. The silence in the room was deafening, as if even the walls were holding their breath. He sat in the suffocating stillness, his mind spinning in circles, replaying the events that had led him to this point.

He had been a rising star, a fearless journalist with a sharp mind and a hunger for the truth. And somewhere along the way, he had lost sight of his principles, his moral compass thrown off-balance by the need to bring justice. It was that same determination and ability to haggle that got him involved with some savory folk. Those who neither appreciated his intrusive nose up their business nor found even the slightest amusements in his earnest desire to uncover the truth.

And then, the scandal. The fake interview, the tampered evidence. His mind flitted back to the moment when it all came crashing down. He had been summoned to the editor's office, his heart pounding in his chest as he walked through the door.

"Flynn," the editor had said, his face grave. "We've received a tip-off about the Festival Poisoning from the NYPD. Detective Bordeaux claimed that you have been charged guilty of possession and tampering of evidence, as well as stealing from the department."

Marcus had tried to deny it and told them that it was all a lie. That he had done no such thing. But the stolen bags of police evidence found tucked away in his car were enough to set flames to everything he had worked so hard to achieve. He had been framed, and the task had been executed so effortlessly that even he had to remind himself of his innocence.

Now, he was paying the price of his unbridled heroism with every puff of his cigarette and the bitter residue of whiskey at the back of his throat.

He stubbed out the cigarette in an ashtray, the embers sizzling as the last wisps of smoke curled into the air. His fingers drummed absently on the armrest of his chair, a nervous habit he'd developed since the whole ordeal. His eyes drifted to a stack of newspapers on his desk, the headlines blaring his downfall in bold, unforgiving letters. Pushing himself to his feet, the tension in his muscles was palpable as he paced back and forth across the small office. The floorboards creaked under his weight, the faint sound echoing in the silence.

He stopped, staring out of the window at the city street below. It was late afternoon, the shadows lengthening as the sun began to set.

The people on the street seemed small and insignificant, unaware of the chaos that had consumed his life.

He clenched his jaw, his hands curling into fists at his sides. He had to do something; he had to find a way to clear his name.

This was how he, in all his red-haired and perpetual scowl glory, came to find out about the LHC. He made it his life's mission to get to the bottom of it. If he could uncover something big, it could surely help him steer both his career and his life back in order.

* * *

A lone fly buzzed against the dusty windowpane of John's cabin. Outside, the Wyoming pines swayed gently in the afternoon breeze, a stark contrast to the turmoil brewing inside the retired Colonel. John, a man sculpted by years of military discipline, sat hunched over a cluttered desk, a worn copy of a scientific journal splayed open in front of him.

He wasn't your typical retiree. His weathered face, etched with the map lines of a thousand covert operations, held a steely focus as he reread a passage about the Large Hadron Collider or LHC. He had spent the last few years utilizing his unique skillset - a blend of tactical expertise and intelligence analysis - to consult on security at some of the world's most high-profile science facilities, including the LHC itself. But recently, a creeping unease had begun to gnaw at him.

The official narrative, the one he helped secure, painted the LHC as a revolutionary tool for understanding the universe, a machine probing the fundamental building blocks of reality. Yet, the deeper John delved into the technical jargon, the more dissonance he felt. Terms like "extra dimensions" and "parallel universes" danced before his eyes, concepts that seemed to be ripped straight from science fiction.

A creak on the wooden floorboards sent John's head snapping up. He grabbed the worn M1911 pistol that lay beside his keyboard, a conditioned reflex from his days in the field. The intruder, however, was far less menacing. Max, his scruffy sheepdog, trotted in, tail wagging, a muddy tennis ball clenched in his teeth. John chuckled, holstering the weapon.

"Alright, alright, boy," he said, scratching Max behind the ears. "We can discuss existential dread later. Fetch?"

Max dropped the ball at John's feet with a happy bark. As John tossed it, the worn leather of the ball caught the glint of the afternoon sun, momentarily reflecting the symbol of the LHC - a ring of interlocking circles. The symbol felt like a mocking reminder, a portal to a world of unknowns that John, for the first time in his life, wasn't sure he wanted to explore. He had always prided himself on his ability to see through the fog of war, to understand the bigger picture. Now, gazing at the symbol, a chilling suspicion began to form. Maybe the biggest lie wasn't being told to the public but to himself. Maybe the fog of war had simply morphed into a different kind of mist, a scientific one, obscuring a truth far more unsettling than any battlefield he'd ever faced.

He picked up the journal again, his gaze hardening. He wouldn't let this go. He was Colonel John Harris, and he wouldn't rest until he understood the real purpose of the machine he'd helped secure. The hunt for truth, it seemed, wasn't about to end with retirement.

John gripped the steering wheel of his beat-up pickup truck, knuckles white. The rhythmic drumming of rain against the windshield mirrored the nervous tremor in his hands. He glanced at the worn leather satchel beside him, the lockpicks nestled within a silent promise of what was to come. Tonight, he was infiltrating a facility that made the warzones he'd traversed seem like playgrounds.

The GPS led him down a desolate stretch of highway, the only light source the occasional flicker of distant lightning. Finally, he pulled onto a dusty side road, the headlights illuminating a towering complex that seemed to rise out of the night like a malevolent metal monolith. This was it: the American arm of the LHC project, a sprawling network of buildings secured with a level of paranoia that would make even the Pentagon blush.

John's heart hammered a frantic rhythm against his ribs. He'd spent weeks meticulously planning this operation, aided by the cryptic yet invaluable intel from his newly formed online alliance - a hacker with the moniker "Phoenix." Phoenix had provided detailed blueprints of the facility's security grid and vulnerability maps and even managed to disable a few key access points remotely. But John knew the real challenge lay ahead - infiltrating the core research labs, the heart of the project.

Taking a deep breath, John donned a nondescript black jacket and a worn baseball cap, pulling it low over his forehead. He exited the truck, his boots crunching on the gravel path. The air crackled with a nervous energy, the silence broken only by the relentless howl of the wind. John moved with the practiced stealth of a predator, years of muscle memory kicking in. He scaled a chain-link fence with surprising agility for a man his age, adrenaline coursing through his veins.

He found himself in a network of dimly lit corridors snaking through the complex's underbelly. Following Phoenix's instructions, he navigated the labyrinthine passageways, his senses on high alert. The only sounds were the rhythmic drip of condensation and the distant hum of unseen machinery. He reached a heavily secured door, its surface emblazoned with a glowing red access panel.

John's fingers danced across the worn leather satchel, feeling the reassuring weight of the lockpicks. He expertly manipulated the tools, with years of experience guiding his movements. With a satisfying click, the lock yielded. He slipped inside, with his heart pounding against his ribs.

The room was a stark contrast to the drab corridors outside. Rows of glowing computer monitors displayed a dizzying array of complex data streams. Scientists with harried expressions hunched over lab benches, their faces illuminated by the eerie blue light of the monitors. This was the heart of the operation, the place where the secrets of reality were being unlocked or, perhaps, tampered with.

But John's attention was drawn to a separate area partitioned by a bulletproof glass wall. Inside, a team of engineers diligently worked on a machine unlike anything he'd ever seen. It was a colossal apparatus, a twisted metal labyrinth that pulsed with an otherworldly energy. A cold dread settled in John's stomach. This wasn't just about probing the universe's fundamental building blocks. This machine, he could feel it in his gut, was designed to do something far more ominous, something that could potentially tear the very fabric of reality apart.

John straightened, a newfound resolve hardening his gaze. He had stumbled upon something far bigger than he could have ever imagined. The fight for truth, it seemed, had just reached a terrifying new level.

***

The rhythmic clatter of Manchester rain against the corrugated metal roof served as a monotonous soundtrack to Zara Akhter's furious typing. Hunched over a battered laptop in her cramped Karachi apartment, she weaved through layers of corporate firewalls with the practiced ease of a seasoned climber scaling a familiar mountain. Tonight's target: Zarka Industries, a seemingly innocuous Karachi-based tech firm rumored to be a front for another cult-like group's ever-expanding influence in Pakistan.

Zara, a young woman barely out of her twenties, had short, auburn hair that matched beautifully with the dark circles etched beneath her hazel eyes. Her features, a captivating blend of South Asian and British heritage, were framed by a mane of unruly curls that seemed to mirror the chaos within her. Every keystroke resonated with a quiet fury, a potent mix of grief and defiance.

The memory of her brother, Faisal, flickered across the screen of her mind, superimposed on the lines of code. A talented coder himself, Faisal had been working on a project to expose the environmental hazards of Zarka Industries' waste disposal facility. The "accident" that claimed his life felt suspiciously convenient. She, refusing to believe it was just a tragic coincidence, had vowed to use her exceptional hacking skills to dismantle the corrupt network that had taken her brother away.

Tonight, she was after a specific file: a blueprint for a data encryption algorithm rumored to be used by Zarka Industries to shield their more nefarious activities. With it, she could expose the truth about their environmental violations and potentially link them to the Cabal's web of deceit.

A triumphant grin split her face as she bypassed the final security hurdle. The access granted a glimpse into the company's digital vault, a treasure trove of secrets waiting to be unearthed. But her celebration was short-lived. A system alert flashed on the screen - intrusion detected. Her heart hammered against her ribs. Zarka's security protocols were no joke.

Just as she braced herself for a digital counter-offensive, a new window popped up. Anonymously encrypted, it displayed a single line of text:

Need a hand?

Heart pounding with a mix of apprehension and curiosity, she typed back, "Who's this?"

A moment later, the reply arrived: *Someone who wants to see the Cabal fall just as much as you do.*

Intrigued and faced with a rapidly dwindling window of opportunity, Zara took a deep breath and began to type. Maybe, just maybe, this unexpected help could be the key to exposing the truth and getting one step closer to justice for Faisal. In the dimly lit apartment, illuminated only by the glow of the laptop screen, an unlikely alliance was about to be forged in the digital shadows.

* * *

Meanwhile, the emergency klaxons finally wailed to a halt, replaced by an anxious silence. The crimson anomaly on the monitor pulsed with a diminished intensity, a sickly echo of its former fury. Relief washed over Evelyn in waves, quickly followed by a tide of unease. The shutdown sequence, a desperate Hail Mary, had somehow worked. But how, and at what cost?

Evelyn found Dr. Weiss in his office, a stark contrast to the sterile control room. Bookshelves overflowed with arcane texts alongside cutting-edge scientific journals. Weiss, his once-youthful face now etched with the relentless pursuit of knowledge, looked up from a glowing tablet. His eyes, usually sparkling with scientific curiosity, held a disconcerting glint.

"Evelyn," he greeted, his voice laced with a hint of amusement. "I see the little hiccup has been addressed." His words hung heavy in the air, a stark contrast to the devastation they had just narrowly avoided.

"Hiccup?" Evelyn bristled. "Dr. Weiss, we nearly tore a hole in reality tonight! Do you have any idea what could have happened?"

Weiss chuckled, a dry, humorless sound. "Progress, my dear Evelyn, is rarely a smooth journey. We've achieved what countless others only dared to dream of. A doorway, a peek beyond the veil." His gaze drifted back to the tablet, a predatory gleam in his eyes.

Evelyn felt a surge of anger and betrayal. Weiss, her mentor, the man who had once ignited her passion for science, now seemed consumed by an ambition bordering on madness. "A doorway?" she scoffed. "More like a gaping maw, ready to swallow us whole!"

"A necessary risk, Evelyn," Weiss countered, his voice firm. "The potential rewards are immeasurable. Think of the knowledge, the power we can unlock!" He gestured expansively. "Imagine rewriting the very fabric of reality!"

Evelyn stared at him, a chilling realization dawning. Weiss wasn't afraid of the anomaly; he was enthralled by it. He wasn't a scientist anymore; he was a gambler, and the stakes were the fate of the world.

"This isn't about science, Dr. Weiss," she said, her voice tight with controlled fury. "This is about your own twisted ambition. You're playing with forces you don't understand."

Weiss' smile faltered for a moment, a flicker of doubt clouding his eyes. But then, the glint returned, stronger than before. "Perhaps," he conceded. "But doubt is a luxury we cannot afford. The future lies on the other side of that doorway, Evelyn. And we will be the ones to claim it."

Evelyn left the office, Weiss's words echoing in her ears. The shutdown may have silenced the alarms, but it hadn't quelled the gnawing sense of dread. The anomaly might be subdued, but a more insidious threat loomed within the walls of the LHC. She could feel it in Dr. Wiess' demeanor tonight. Something told her that tearing the reality wasn't the only thing this experiment was capable of doing.

It might be the undoing of their decades-long professional relationship. And should it come to that, she, the reluctant warrior-scientist, knew she'd have to fight back, not just for scientific integrity but for the very survival of humanity.

Back in his office, Dr. Weiss steepled his fingers, his gaze fixed on the holographic display flickering above his desk. The anomaly, once a crimson gash, had shrunk to a pulsating ember, a subdued echo of its former fury. Yet, for Weiss, it remained a beacon, a testament to his audacity and a promise of unimaginable power.

The shutdown sequence, a desperate scramble by the timorous fools he called colleagues, had been a nuisance, a wrinkle in his grand design. But a temporary one. He, unlike them, understood the true potential of the anomaly, the gateway it represented to a universe beyond their wildest dreams. Humanity, in its current state, was a stagnant pond, its potential for progress stifled by its own limitations. This breach, this tear in the veil, offered a chance to evolve, to transcend the shackles of their physical forms.

A self-satisfied smirk played on Weiss' lips. He wasn't just a scientist anymore. He was a visionary, a shepherd leading humanity to its glorious new dawn. The ancient texts lining his shelves, dismissed by his narrow-minded peers as mere curiosities, whispered secrets of forgotten powers, of beings that defied the very laws of physics. These were the forces he sought to harness, the knowledge he craved to unlock.

He tapped a holographic command, and the display shifted, revealing a complex diagram — a web of interconnected symbols and equations that resembled a celestial map. This was his magnum opus, the culmination of years spent deciphering the cryptic messages hidden within the ancient texts. It was the key to unlocking the anomaly's true potential, to channeling its raw energy and bending it to his will.

A thrill of anticipation coursed through him. The shutdown had bought him time, a chance to refine his calculations and delve deeper into the forbidden knowledge. But time was a finite resource. The anomaly pulsed, a festering wound in reality, and with each passing moment, the risk of another uncontrolled breach increased. He needed to act and act swiftly.

He glanced at the clock on the wall. It was past midnight, the corridors of the LHC eerily silent. Perfect. He wouldn't need to worry about prying eyes or the interference of his overly cautious colleagues. With a predatory glint in his eyes, Weiss rose from his chair, the weight of the world, or perhaps a new one entirely, resting on his shoulders. He was Dr. Anton Weiss, the man who dared to peer beyond the veil, and he wouldn't let a group of frightened fools stand in his way. Tonight, he would unlock the secrets of the anomaly, and humanity, under his enlightened leadership, would take its first steps into a glorious new era. A cruel smile stretched across his face, a chilling portent of the ambitions that burned within him, ambitions that teetered on the precipice of godhood and madness.

He had to make a few calls. This was too important to be left for tomorrow morning. Dialing a number, he waited till the line connected, only to mumble a quick, "We must speak" before clicking the phone off. The night was still young, but there was much to do, much to discuss, much to settle, and much to embark on.

Somewhere, in an underground bunker, far away from the eyes of any mortal, a meeting was being conducted. The holographic display pulsed with an erratic rhythm, casting an unsettling glow on the faces gathered around the table. Dr. Anya Petrova, her usually steady hand trembling slightly, adjusted the controls. "The readings are off the charts, Dr. Weiss. It wasn't just a hadron collision; it was a… tear. A tear in the fabric of spacetime itself."

Dr. Weiss' aged face was etched with a mixture of scientific curiosity and a hint of manic glee. As he leaned closer, the silver strands of his hair seemed to vibrate with the energy readings. "Excellent, Anya. Excellent. Show me again."

Helena was cloaked in a luxurious crimson robe that contrasted sharply with the sterile environment and spoke in a voice laced with steely resolve. "This anomaly, Anton. Are you certain it's a doorway and not a disaster?"

Weiss straightened, his gaze locking with Helena's. A spark of something akin to defiance flickered in his eyes. "Disaster or destiny, Helena, that remains to be seen. But one thing is certain: this is a turning point. This tear… it's a bridge. A bridge to the next stage of human evolution."

Anya cleared her throat, her voice laced with unease. "But Dr. Weiss, the energy signature… it's unlike anything we've ever encountered. The potential consequences…"

Weiss scoffed, his voice sharp. "Consequences? We are the Cabal, Anya. We don't shy away from consequences; we embrace them! For millennia, humanity has stagnated. This anomaly is the key. The key to unlocking the secrets of other dimensions, to pushing our species beyond its current limitations."

Helena, a glint of avarice in her eyes, chimed in. "And the key to unimaginable power, Anton. Imagine the financial and political possibilities! Those who control this… this doorway will control the future."

Anya shrunk back, a flicker of fear crossing her features. The idealism that had drawn her to the Cabal in the first place seemed to be curdling into something far more sinister.

"D- Dr. Weiss," she stammered, "what about Dr. Shaw? Her experiment caused this… tear. Shouldn't we at least try to understand it before we…"

Weiss' voice boomed, silencing her. "Evelyn Shaw," he spat, his tone laced with disdain. "A talented student, but too cautious. She lacks the vision the… ruthlessness this endeavor requires. The Cabal will take it from here. We will be the shepherds of this new era, Helena and I. And humanity will kneel before us."

The air crackled with dark energy, a potent mix of ambition, fear, and the chilling certainty that the Cabal, under the leadership of Dr. Weiss and Helena, would stop at nothing to exploit the anomaly for their own twisted ends.

Helena leaned back in her chair, a predatory glint in her eyes. "Evolution, Weiss. You speak of it so grandly. But what exactly do you envision this 'next stage' to be?"

Weiss traced a finger along the holographic display, the chaotic energy tendrils seeming to respond to his touch. "Imagine, Helena. Imagine if we could harness the very essence of this… other dimension. The energy signatures suggest something beyond our comprehension, something that could rewrite the very building blocks of life."

His voice dropped to a conspiratorial whisper. "Imagine human lifespans extended indefinitely. Imagine eradicating disease at its genetic root. Imagine granting ourselves abilities once thought relegated to the realm of science fiction – telekinesis, telepathy, interdimensional travel…"

Unable to contain herself any longer, Anya blurted out, "But Dr. Weiss, tampering with the fundamental laws of physics… it's uncharted territory! The risks are incalculable!"

Weiss spun toward her, his eyes flashing with a dangerous light. "Risks are for the faint of heart, Anya. The potential rewards here are beyond anything humanity has ever dreamed of. This anomaly is a gift, a shortcut to an evolutionary leap that would take us millennia to achieve organically."

Helena steepled her fingers, a thoughtful look on her face. "So, how do we proceed? This tear… how do we stabilize it, study it, and most importantly, exploit it?"

Weiss, a predatory smile twisting his lips, began to outline a plan. "We need a two-pronged approach, Helena. First, we need more data. Anya, you will lead a team to delve deeper into the anomaly's properties. See if we can establish a controlled connection, a way to send probes, perhaps even… something more."

Anya gulped, a knot of dread forming in her stomach. The idea of sending something, or someone, through such an unstable rift sent shivers down her spine.

"And secondly," Weiss continued, his voice hardening, "we need to secure this location. No word of this anomaly can ever reach the outside world. Imagine the chaos governments would unleash if they knew about this. We need to control the narrative, Helena. We need to control the future."

Helena nodded with a ruthless glint in her eyes. "Discretion is our watchword, Anton. I will ensure our little… project remains a secret. But securing this location… that might require some… forceful persuasion."

A dark understanding passed between them. The Cabal wasn't known for its gentle touch. The anomaly, a potential key to unimaginable power, had ignited a spark in their hearts, a spark that could very well consume not just them but the world around them in its fiery wake. As Anya, her face pale with a mixture of fear and reluctant fascination, began to formulate a research plan, and Helena plotted the ruthless acquisition of the facility, the fate of humanity teetered on a knife's edge, held aloft by the ambition of two figures willing to break the world in order to remake it.

* * *

Dr. Evelyn clutched a mug of lukewarm coffee, the warmth a meager comfort against the icy dread that had settled in her gut. Across from her, young Thomas, the ever-enthusiastic technician, practically vibrated with excitement. His usually messy brown hair was tamed with an unusual amount of gel, and his eyes shone with a fervor that made Evelyn uneasy.

"Dr. Evelyn," he babbled, his voice barely above a whisper, "the readings… they're unlike anything we've ever seen before! A dimensional tear… a bridge to another reality! Can you believe it?"

Beside him, Nadia, a recent physics graduate with a penetrating gaze, leaned forward. "Excuse me, Dr. Evelyn, but… could you explain what happened in simpler terms? I understand the basics of the LHC, but this… this tear you mentioned…"

Evelyn sighed, the weight of the situation pressing down on her. "Yes, Nadia," she began, her voice raspy. "During the experiment, something… unexpected happened. The particle collision triggered something far beyond what we were anticipating. Our instruments picked up readings that defied explanation. It's… as if we ripped a hole in the very fabric of reality."

A shiver ran down her spine as the memory of the blinding flash, the surge of chaotic energy, slammed into her. Thomas, oblivious to her distress, continued to chatter excitedly about potential applications, about rewriting the laws of physics, about achieving human immortality.

Evelyn forced a smile. "It's a fascinating anomaly, Thomas. But we need to be cautious. We don't understand the ramifications of such a breach. This could be a groundbreaking discovery, or it could be a catastrophic event."

A shadow flickered across her face, a memory surfacing from the depths of her mind. Her mother, a brilliant physicist herself, had vanished without a trace ten years ago. There had been whispers of a secret project at the LHC, a project her mother had been deeply involved in. Could it be connected, somehow, to this anomaly?

Evelyn pushed the thought away. Now wasn't the time for morbid speculation. She needed to focus on containment, on ensuring this tear didn't widen and unleash whatever horrors lurked on the other side.

As she spoke, outlining a plan for further investigation with a heavy dose of caution, a new resolve hardened within her. This anomaly, this tear in reality, wasn't just a scientific curiosity anymore.

It was a personal quest, a desperate attempt to understand what happened to her mother and, perhaps, to prevent a similar fate for the world they knew.

Nadia, ever the pragmatist, interjected with a pointed question. "Dr. Shaw, shouldn't we inform Dr. Weiss about this anomaly? Surely, his experience and expertise would be invaluable in…"

Evelyn's hand tightened around her mug, the warmth a stark contrast to the sudden chill that crept down her spine. The mere mention of Dr. Weiss sent a tremor of unease through her. His earlier visit, filled with barely veiled excitement and a disturbing glint in his eyes as he spoke of the anomaly's potential, had left her feeling like a pawn in a game she didn't understand.

"There's… t- time," she stammered, forcing a smile that didn't quite reach her eyes. "This anomaly is unlike anything we've encountered. We need to solidify our data and understand its properties before we bring in anyone else."

The truth, a truth she couldn't quite articulate, was that Dr. Weiss's ambition, his hunger for groundbreaking discoveries, felt… unsettling. There was a darkness behind his enthusiasm, a hint of something far more sinister than pure scientific curiosity.

Evelyn wasn't naive. She knew the Cabal existed, a shadowy network of scientists rumored to push the boundaries of ethics in their pursuit of knowledge. Dr. Weiss, with his past shrouded in secrecy and his ruthless approach to research had always been a name whispered in hushed tones in connection with the Cabal.

Could it be a coincidence? Was Dr. Weiss' sudden interest in the anomaly just a thirst for groundbreaking research, or was there something more at play? A cold dread settled in her stomach. The anomaly, once a fascinating scientific puzzle, now felt like a ticking time bomb, and she wasn't sure who to trust with its detonation.

Nadia, sensing Evelyn's hesitation, pressed on gently. "But Dr. Evelyn, with all due respect, this is bigger than any of us. The implications of a dimensional tear…"

"I understand, Nadia," Evelyn interrupted, her voice firm despite the tremor in her heart. "But trust me, for now, this needs to be contained. We need a plan, a way to approach this anomaly cautiously and ethically. Once we have a better understanding, then we can decide who to involve."

A tense silence descended upon the room. Evelyn knew Nadia wasn't entirely convinced, but for now, she had managed to buy some time. Time to delve deeper, time to understand the anomaly, and, most importantly, time to figure out who she could truly trust in this unsettling game of scientific discovery with potentially world-ending consequences. The weight of the secret, the fear of the unknown, and the nagging suspicion about Dr. Weiss gnawed at her. Evelyn knew, with a chilling certainty, that this anomaly was just the beginning, and the path ahead was fraught with peril.

The fluorescent lights of the lab buzzed overhead, casting a sterile glow on the three figures huddled around the holographic display of the anomaly. Thomas, his youthful enthusiasm barely contained, bounced on the balls of his feet.

"So, Dr. Shaw," he blurted, his voice brimming with barely suppressed excitement, "what do you think caused the flash? A tear in reality... it's mind-blowing! Maybe..." he lowered his voice to a conspiratorial whisper, "maybe it was... them."

Nadia, ever the grounded one, arched an eyebrow. "Them? Who's them, Thomas?"

Thomas' eyes gleamed. "Aliens, Nadia! Extraterrestrials! Imagine a whole other dimension, teeming with life! Maybe this tear... maybe it's a doorway they opened, trying to reach us!"

Nadia snorted, a hint of amusement battling with the seriousness of the situation. "Aliens, Thomas? Really? While the concept is fascinating, wouldn't a more... terrestrial explanation be more likely?"

Evelyn, her mind a whirlwind of thoughts, remained silent. The idea of aliens, though fantastical, resonated with a deep unease within her. The memory of the blinding flash, the surge of chaotic energy, flickered behind her eyelids. It wasn't just a tear; it felt... hostile, like a hungry maw reaching out from another reality.

A new wave of dread washed over her. What if Thomas was right, not about aliens specifically, but about something... else... coming through the tear? What if this wasn't a bridge but a gaping wound spewing forth horrors from beyond their comprehension?

She forced herself to focus, pushing aside the chilling possibilities. "Let's not get ahead of ourselves," she said, her voice surprisingly steady. "The anomaly is a tear, yes, but whether it's a doorway or not, we don't know. Our priority right now is containment. We need to understand its properties, find a way to stabilize it before..." her voice trailed off, the unspoken fear hanging heavy in the air.

Nadia, her youthful idealism tinged with a newfound seriousness, spoke up. "But Dr. Shaw, what if this… tear… what if it's already spewing something out? What if there are… consequences we haven't considered?"

The weight of Nadia's question settled on them like a lead weight. Evelyn, her heart pounding against her ribs, knew Nadia was right. The ethical implications of this discovery were staggering. Did they have the right to tamper with the fabric of reality, even if it meant potential breakthroughs for science? And what if their actions unleashed a catastrophe they couldn't contain?

As Thomas continued to babble excitedly about alien civilizations and interdimensional travel, a steely resolve hardened within Evelyn. This wasn't just about scientific discovery anymore. It was about protecting their world, about closing the Pandora's Box they had inadvertently opened. She needed a plan, a way to approach this anomaly with both caution and a sense of urgency. A plan that didn't involve Dr. Weiss and his unsettling hunger for groundbreaking results, no matter the cost.

Looking at her two colleagues, their faces etched with a mixture of excitement and trepidation, Evelyn knew they were in this together. They were the first line of defense, the guardians standing between their reality and whatever lurked on the other side of the tear.

Somewhere, onwards to the cold mounts of North Dakota, retired Colonel John turned up the collar of his jacket to dispel some of the cold that threatened to seep into his bones. Even Max was curled up on the passenger seat with a blanket over him. He wondered where his military honor and the need to protect his country would lead him. Would he ever confront this elusive cult, or would he lose his life trying?

Elsewhere, Manchester continued to weep as Zara Akhtar, a sheet wrapped around her head, knelt on her mat. It was a brief break from the clickity-clack of her keyboard. Prayer was the only thing that gave her some semblance of hope. In a world where everything felt so temporary, the only things that seemed to feel close to eternal were spirituality and the binary. And for those few minutes, with her hands raised in supplication, neither the digital warfare mattered nor did vengeance.

She thought of Faisal once more. How he used to strive for justice, never once fearing the consequences. He was her idol, the one she looked up to in her moments of weakness, the one she sought for guidance. Their parents had molded both their children with the tough love only Eurasians knew. And she was grateful for that, thankful that it made her the independent individual she was today.

With a heavy sigh, she prayed that the fellow cyber-terrorist she had recently encountered would be the ally she needed to move in with her plan of bringing the Cabal down. They had not only been working their influence through the field of education but also had dipped their toe in both the healthcare and technological sectors of today's insanely globalized world.

Turning the corner to what could only be described as nowhere, Marcus Flynn stuffed his hands into the pockets of his pants. He walked aimlessly, trying to clear his head. The LHC, something he had recovered from folders an ex-colleague had sent over weeks ago, was the only thought that coveted his mind. He wondered where he should start and what even were the implications of such a project.

The government base was situated some few miles East of Fargo, and he knew he needed a guise to get in. After all, no one wanted a muck-faced journalist snooping on their work.

Who did he know that could have links to something like that? He thought for a while, leaning against the wall of a dirty alleyway. The stench of piled garbage, combined with that of urine and just overall gunk, was a less-than-glamorous companion to his thoughts.

"North Dakota…North Dakota," he muttered to himself, scrolling through the contacts in his phone.

He could try Johannes; he worked somewhere in State Affairs and might have an insight.

He shook his head as if dispelling the thought. He could be a good source, but not his main one.

Who else?

Using his free hand to massage his temples, he groaned and grumbled something about never having the right people when he needed them. Just as he was about to give up and give Johannes a call, a notification from an extended family group caught his attention. His wife, Maisie, had always tried to get involved with the whole 'family sticks together' thing, even if he were the last person who wanted to uphold that ideology.

Nevertheless, he clicked on it. It wasn't something remarkable. Just one of Maisie's uncles having sent a picture of his kids talking about how he missed the event the picture had been clicked at. Aldo added something about one of his daughters being gone to Fargo for work. Marcus rolled his eyes at the distraction, even if the sight of family interaction made him think of all the people, both whom he had pushed away and those who had distanced themselves willingly after his scandal. Just as he was about to exit the group chat, something caught his eye.

It was the profile picture said daughter had, adorning a graduation robe with the monogram of a prestigious academy for science and technology.

He pursed his lips, thinking this through. She might know something. Science, Fargo; she seemed to be around the perimeter of where he wanted to go. Taking a deep breath, he singled out her contact and gave her a text. Short, simple, and precise.

Call me. Need to chat about something important.

This was going to be slow, and he knew it, but it was his best chance at doing what he needed to clear his name.

Unbeknownst to them all, as they went about their lives beneath the same skies, a flash of unbridled energy streaked across the clouds. It was quick, gone before most could even acknowledge it. But its presence was insidious, one that would surely return to haunt their waking realities. Now, whether they were those who sought to rid the world of such a disparity should it befall or those who wished to harness its power for their own gain, one thing was inevitable.

They were all tied together in this, regardless of their intentions.

Chapter 2: Echoes of the Past

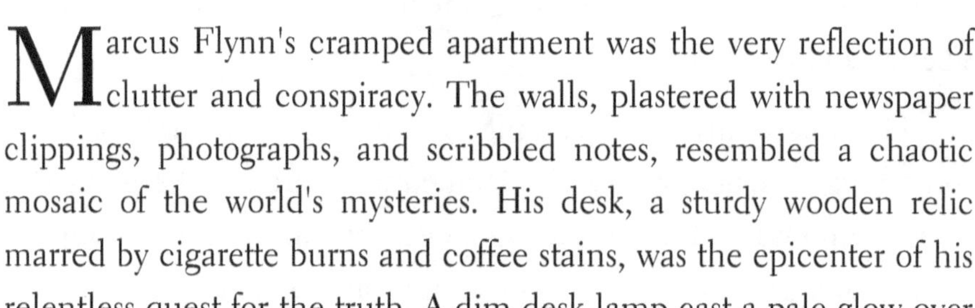

Marcus Flynn's cramped apartment was the very reflection of clutter and conspiracy. The walls, plastered with newspaper clippings, photographs, and scribbled notes, resembled a chaotic mosaic of the world's mysteries. His desk, a sturdy wooden relic marred by cigarette burns and coffee stains, was the epicenter of his relentless quest for the truth. A dim desk lamp cast a pale glow over stacks of documents and a humming laptop.

He slumped in his chair, fingers drumming on the table, eyes glued to the screen. The glow of the city seeped through the half-drawn blinds, painting stripes of light and shadow across his furrowed face. He was exhausted, but the kind of tiredness that fuels a relentless mind. He'd been deep in research for hours, sifting through obscure scientific journals, encrypted government files, and bizarre online forums.

The LHC, or Large Hadron Collider, was the latest knot in the web of intrigue that Marcus was determined to untangle. He took a sip of his lukewarm coffee, grimacing at the bitter taste. Though he'd never admit it out loud, he missed the way Maisie brewed it for him every morning before their fallout.

Nevertheless, his laptop screen displayed a series of articles about unexplained global disruptions—freak weather patterns, unexplained animal behavior, and reports of strange lights in the sky. To most, these events were unrelated oddities. To Marcus, they were pieces of a puzzle.

Suddenly, his phone buzzed, shattering the silence. He glanced at the screen—Nadia, his wife's niece, was calling. Marcus had reached out to her earlier that week, intrigued by her recent move to North Dakota for a government job in the "science field."

"Afternoon, Nadia," he answered, his voice a mix of fatigue and anticipation.

"Hi, Uncle Mark," came her voice, crisp and detached, the kind of professional tone that one would associate with a recent graduate trying to make a mark in her field. "I got your message. What's this about?"

Marcus leaned back, running a hand through his disheveled ginger hair. "I'm looking into some strange occurrences, and I came across something about a research facility in North Dakota. You wouldn't happen to know anything about that, would you?"

There was a pause, a hesitation that made his heart skip a beat. "There is a government research facility here," Nadia said carefully. "We're working on... physics, mostly."

"Physics, huh?" Marcus leaned forward, sensing an opening. "Anything to do with particle collisions? Maybe a certain collider?"

"Look, Uncle Mark, I can't discuss the specifics. It's classified." Her voice was edged with discomfort, a rigid shield against his probing. "But yes, there is some advanced research going on."

"Advanced research..." Marcus echoed, his mind racing. "Nadia, you've got to give me more than that. I'm onto something big, and I need to know if this facility is involved."

Nadia sighed, a sound of resignation. "All I can say is that there are projects here that involve more than just theoretical physics. But that's all, okay? I could get into serious trouble for even hinting at this."

"Got it. Thanks, kid," Marcus said, his voice softening. "Stay safe, okay?"

"Yeah, you too." With that, the line went dead, leaving Marcus in a state of silence and intrigue.

He stared at the phone, then back at his laptop, the dots beginning to connect in his mind. Marcus' fingers flew over the keyboard, diving deeper into the digital abyss. He hacked through layers of reports and amateur recordings of said 'anomalies,' piecing together snippets of information that painted a chilling picture. Reports of energy fluctuations, sudden disappearances, and encrypted communications suggested something far beyond ordinary science.

He swiveled in his chair, his heart still pounding from his conversation with Nadia. His mind raced with the implications of what he had just uncovered. The revelation that the LHC could be a portal to other dimensions was both thrilling and terrifying. But now, he needed to dig deeper. He needed to find out if the global disruptions he had been tracking were connected to the LHC's experiments.

The LHC is just a particle collider, he told himself. The rumors about it being a portal, a doorway to other dimensions, hidden away in the vast emptiness of North Dakota, seemed too sci-fi cliché for his taste.

The hum of his laptop was a constant companion as he navigated through layers of data, documents, and encrypted files. His apartment, dimly lit and cluttered with the detritus of a life consumed by conspiracy, seemed to close in around him as he delved further into the mystery. He opened a fresh pot of coffee, the bitter aroma filling the room, and set his mind to the task at hand.

He started by creating a timeline on a large sheet of paper pinned to the wall. He jotted down dates, locations, and descriptions of the anomalies he had come across in his research. There were reports of strange lights in the sky, odd weather patterns, and unexplained sonic booms that had been cropping up all over the world in the past week.

He recalled a recent news article about a mysterious flash of light over the Australian outback that had baffled scientists and left residents spooked. There were similar reports from across the globe—northern Canada, the Sahara Desert, and even the Himalayas. Each event seemed to occur in remote, sparsely populated areas, making them easier to dismiss as natural phenomena or isolated incidents.

The first anomaly Marcus investigated was the unexplained flash of light over the Australian outback. He pulled up satellite imagery and weather reports from the region, poring over the data for any clues. The light had been described as a blinding flash, lasting just a few seconds but visible for miles. There had been no thunderstorm activity in the area, and no meteor showers were expected at that time.

Marcus' eyes narrowed as he read through eyewitness accounts. People had reported seeing a brilliant, pulsating light that seemed to hover in the sky before suddenly disappearing. Some described feeling a strange sense of vertigo or disorientation during the event. He cross-referenced these reports with data from seismic sensors and found a minor tremor recorded at the exact time of the flash.

"Interesting..." he muttered to himself, scribbling notes on his timeline. A minor earthquake in conjunction with the flash suggested an intense release of energy. But from what source? He made a mental note to look into geological activities that could explain such an event.

Next, Marcus turned his attention to the reports of sonic booms in the Sahara Desert. These had been occurring sporadically for the past week with no apparent cause. He pulled up audio recordings from weather stations and analyzed the waveforms. The booms were loud, almost deafening, and appeared to come from high in the atmosphere.

He compared the timing of these booms with the operations schedule of the LHC. He delved into scientific forums and databases, looking for explanations that could tie these anomalies to the collider's experiments. There were some theories about high-energy particles interacting with the atmosphere, but nothing conclusive. Marcus noted down the details, his mind racing with possibilities.

Finally, Marcus turned his attention to the Himalayas, where reports of bizarre weather patterns had been emerging. In one instance, a sudden, intense storm appeared out of nowhere, dumping several feet of snow in a matter of hours. What made this even more unusual was that the storm had formed in an area that had been clear and calm just minutes before.

Marcus reviewed satellite images and weather data, looking for anything that might explain this anomaly. The storm had indeed appeared suddenly, with no warning. The temperature had plummeted, and wind speeds had reached hurricane force within minutes.

He leaned back in his chair, rubbing his temples. The connections were becoming clearer, but the implications were staggering. There wasn't much info on the LHC that he could use to understand how deep those implications of 'secret government experiments' went.

If he were to believe that it was the LHC causing this and *if* he further humored the idea of interdimensional traveling and aliens and all that junk, then it wasn't just opening portals—it was causing disruptions that could be felt across the globe. The idea that these anomalies were linked to the collider's experiments was both exhilarating and frightening.

Marcus turned his attention back to the timeline on the wall. He circled the key dates and locations, connecting the dots with a red string. The picture that emerged was one of a world on the brink of extraordinary change, with the LHC at the center of it all. The boundaries between science and mysticism were blurred, and Marcus was determined to uncover the truth, no matter the cost.

He stood up, stretching his aching muscles, and stared at the timeline. Each anomaly, each flash of light, and each sonic boom was a clue pointing toward a hidden reality. The world was changing, and Marcus Flynn was on the front lines of the discovery. The journey ahead was fraught with danger, but he knew he had to press on. The truth was out there, and he was closer than ever to uncovering it.s

With a deep breath, he sat back down at his desk. He had a lot more research to do. The anomalies were just the beginning. He needed to find out what was really happening at the LHC and why the world was starting to feel the effects of its alleged experiments. He opened another document, ready to dive back into the mystery, driven by a relentless need to know the truth.

It had been over eight hours, countless cigarettes, and an alarming lack of bathroom breaks when he finally admitted that his research had led him to a dead end. He knew that if he wanted to dig deeper into the secrets of the LHC, he needed help. Not the kind you find in academic circles or on public forums but the kind that thrived in the shadows of the digital world.

With a sigh, he reached for his phone and scrolled through his contacts, landing on a name that sent a shiver down his spine: Shade. Shade was a hacker with a reputation for diving into the darkest corners of the internet, where morals and laws were merely suggestions. Marcus had crossed paths with him once before during an investigation into corporate espionage. Shade had helped him then, and now Marcus needed his expertise again.

He dialed the number, his heart pounding in his chest. After a few rings, a gruff voice answered, "Shade."

"It's Marcus Flynn," he said, trying to keep his voice steady. "I need your help. It's urgent."

There was a pause, then a low chuckle. "Well, well, if it isn't the truth-seeker himself. What kind of trouble are you stirring up now, Flynn?"

Marcus quickly explained his findings and his suspicions about the LHC. Shade listened in silence, the only sound being the occasional click of a keyboard on the other end of the line.

"Alright," Shade finally said. "This sounds big and dangerous. I'll help, but it's gonna cost you."

"Name your price," Marcus replied, desperation seeping into his voice.

"First, I'll need you to run a program I'll send over. It'll cloak your digital footprint. You don't want anyone tracing you when you visit the places I'm sending you to."

Marcus felt a knot tighten in his stomach. "What kind of places?"

"Dark web stuff. Places where the line between friend and foe is a fine one. Post your issue there, and if you're lucky, someone might help you. Or they might ruin you. Your call."

A few minutes later, Marcus received an email from a strange account, which he assumed was one of Shade's, with an attachment and a set of instructions. He downloaded the file and ran the program, watching as his laptop's screen flickered and then displayed a series of cryptic symbols. The program hummed to life, encrypting his data and masking his IP address.

"Alright, you're good to go," Shade said over the phone. "Check your email again. I've sent you a link to a site called 'The Abyss.' Post your issue there and see what bites. But be careful, Flynn. The people on this site are not to be trifled with."

"Thanks, Shade," Marcus said, his voice wavering with both gratitude and fear.

"Don't thank me yet," Shade replied with a dark chuckle. "Just watch your back."

Marcus hung up and took a deep breath. He clicked on the link Shade had sent and was greeted by a stark, black webpage with a simple message: "Never Blink When the Abyss Stares Back at You." He navigated through the site, past layers of cryptic messages and hidden forums, until he found a section titled "Inquiries."

He hesitated for a moment, then typed out a brief message:

Subject: *Need Information on LHC Experiments*

> *I'm looking for information about recent activities at the Large Hadron Collider. Specifically interested in any secret experiments or anomalies linked to global disruptions. Any insights would be greatly appreciated.*

He hit send and leaned back, his heart pounding in his chest. Now, all he could do was wait.

It didn't take long. Within minutes, a notification popped up. A response from a user named "Phoenix."

>Phoenix

I have some information. Join the private channel I've set up for you. We'll talk there. Be quick.

Marcus clicked on the link Phoenix provided, and a new window opened, leading to a private chatroom. His hands trembled as he typed.

>BigRedStud

I'm here. What do you have?

There was a pause, then a flurry of messages from Phoenix.

>Phoenix

The LHC is not what it seems. It's a gateway. They've been conducting experiments that are related to the Cabal; I have files that prove it. Sending them now. Use caution. This information is dangerous.

A file transfer request popped up on Marcus' screen. He accepted, and his laptop began to download a series of encrypted files. He could feel his heart racing as the progress bar crept forward.

>Phoenix

These files will give you the truth, but be warned. They will also put a target on your back. Don't trust anyone. Especially those who claim to be on your side.

With that, Phoenix signed off, leaving Marcus alone with his thoughts and the ominous files now sitting on his desktop.

He stared at the screen, a sense of foreboding washing over him. He had what he needed, but at what cost? The truth was within his grasp, but the dangers that came with it were becoming all too real. With a deep breath, he began to open the files, bracing himself for whatever revelations lay ahead.

He clicked on a file marked "Project Gateway," his heart pounding in his chest. The document detailed experiments that went beyond the bounds of known physics, involving the manipulation of space-time and access to parallel universes. The implications were staggering—if the LHC was indeed a portal, it could explain the global disruptions he'd been tracking.

Then there was the mention of the Cabal, this scientology kind of cult that seemed to have its toes dipped in every major corporation behind the scenes.

Marcus leaned back, staring at the screen in disbelief. He was on the brink of a discovery that could shake the foundations of science and reality itself. The LHC, hidden beneath the plains of North Dakota, was more than just a scientific marvel; it was a Pandora's box, and someone had thrown open the lid.

First, he tried to match the files' information with the globally occurring incidents. There was a curious correlation; each sonic boom coincided with a major energy surge at the collider. The realization sent a chill down Marcus' spine. If the LHC was truly creating portals, it could be that these booms were the result of sudden releases of energy as these portals opened or closed. He cross-referenced this event with the LHC's operations and, once again, found a correlation. The storm had occurred during a time when the collider was undergoing a major experiment.

The sound of distant sirens wailing in the night pulled Marcus from his thoughts. The world outside continued to spin, oblivious to the seismic shifts that lurked beneath the surface. But Marcus knew. He had seen the first glimpse of a truth that could change everything, and there was no turning back.

With a determined glint in his eye, he saved the files and powered down his laptop. The journey to uncover the full scope of the LHC's secrets had only just begun, and Marcus Flynn was ready to face whatever lay on the other side of the portal.

* * *

Dr. Evelyn Shaw sat at her untidy desk, the hum of machinery creating a background of white noise in the stark, sterile environment. Around her, a chaotic assortment of diagrams, reports, and computer screens displayed data that painted a grim picture. The world was in upheaval, and the anomalies spreading across the globe were evidence of a reality that was no longer behaving as it should.

The experiment conducted last week with the Large Hadron Collider had pushed the boundaries of known science and, in doing so, had torn through the very fabric of the universe. Evelyn's pragmatic and fiercely intelligent mind worked overtime as she sifted through the data, seeking a solution to the crisis they had inadvertently unleashed.

A hesitant knock on the door broke her concentration. Looking up, she saw Nadia, a fresh-faced graduate who had only recently joined the team. Nadia had been brimming with enthusiasm when she arrived, eager to contribute to the groundbreaking work being done here. Now, however, her expression was one of apprehension as she clutched a stack of new reports.

"Dr. Shaw, I have the latest updates," Nadia said, her voice tinged with nervousness. She handed over the documents, her hands shaking slightly. "The anomalies…they're spreading faster than we anticipated. We're getting new reports from all over the world."

Evelyn took the papers, quickly scanning the data with a furrowed brow. She motioned for Nadia to sit, the young recruit hesitantly taking a seat across from her. The reports detailed a series of bizarre events—a sudden, unexplainable storm in the Sahara, sonic booms in the Arctic, and a dazzling light show over South

America. The anomalies were no longer isolated incidents; they were a global phenomenon.

"Thank you, Nadia," Evelyn said, her voice steady despite the mounting tension. She flipped through the pages, each one reinforcing the severity of their situation. "The experiment has caused breaches in the fabric of reality. These anomalies are the result of those breaches, and they're getting worse."

Nadia, her face pale but determined, leaned forward. "What can we do, Dr. Shaw? How do we stop this?"

Evelyn rose from her chair, her mind racing through the possibilities. "First, we need to shut down the collider immediately. We can't afford to let any more breaches occur. Then, we need to analyze the data from the experiment and figure out exactly where things went wrong. We'll have to isolate and contain the affected areas to prevent further anomalies."

Nadia nodded, her fear giving way to a resolve born from a sense of duty. She had come here to be part of something greater, and now she was facing a challenge that could define her career. "I'll gather the team and contact the authorities. They need to know what we're dealing with."

Evelyn placed a reassuring hand on Nadia's shoulder. "Good. We're going to need everyone's help to get through this. And remember, this is more than just a scientific anomaly. This is a threat to the very fabric of our reality."

Nadia took a deep breath, her determination clear despite the gravity of the situation she faced. She stood up, ready to relay Dr.

Shaw's orders to the rest of the team and to contact the necessary authorities.

As the door closed behind Nadia, Evelyn turned back to her desk, her mind filled with the enormity of the task ahead. She picked up a photograph of the man who was once not only a mentor but also a hero of sorts, Dr. Anton Weiss, who had recently been very rigidly against even the implication of any ethical responsibilities that came with scientific discovery. His crude words echoed in her mind as she prepared for the next steps.

Evelyn knew that shutting down the collider was only the beginning. They would need to stabilize the breaches and mend the fabric of reality itself. The stakes had never been higher, and she felt the weight of the world resting on her shoulders. With a deep breath, she gathered her reports and headed toward the control room, her resolve steeled for the monumental challenge that lay ahead. The anomalies were a sign that reality was in peril, and Evelyn Shaw was determined to do whatever it took to protect the world from the consequences of their scientific ambition. As she walked through the sterile corridors of the facility, she knew that the fate of the universe rested in their hands, and she was ready to fight for it.

She strode with determination through the sleek, white-walled corridors of the North Dakota research facility. The stakes had never been higher; the anomalies caused by their experiment were escalating, threatening to unravel the very fabric of reality. Her destination was the collider control room, where the colossal machine that had pierced the dimensions was being attended to. She had to ensure it was shut down before any more damage could be done.

As she approached the control room, raised voices indicated a heated argument. Upon entering, she found a scene of tension. Thomas, the enthusiastic young engineer with wild, curly brown hair, was in the middle of an argument with Nadia, whose otherwise dusky face was now flushed with frustration.

Jeremiah, a seasoned veteran with a mechanic's expertise, stood nearby, his broad chest crossed by powerful arms. His expression was stony, and he radiated his usual air of authority.

"Jeremiah, what's happening here?" Evelyn's voice cut through the noise, demanding attention.

Thomas turned to her, his eyes filled with a mixture of excitement and frustration. "Dr. Shaw, Nadia insists that we need to shut down the collider immediately. However, we have explicit orders from Dr. Weiss to continue repairs and get the machine back online. We can't just stop now!"

Nadia stepped forward, her voice resolute. "Dr. Shaw, the anomalies are spreading, and they're worsening by the hour. If we don't shut it down now, we could be facing a catastrophe!"

Evelyn's gaze hardened as she addressed Jeremiah. "Dr. Weiss isn't here, and the consequences of continuing this experiment are far too dangerous. We need to shut it down."

Jeremiah's jaw tightened. He raised a large hand, silencing her. "With all due respect, Dr. Shaw, we've received an official directive from Dr. Weiss. This work is to proceed, no exceptions."

Evelyn's frustration grew. She knew Dr. Weiss's reputation for prioritizing scientific progress over safety and ethical considerations.

"Jeremiah, you know the risks. The anomalies are a direct result of the experiment. We can't afford to continue and risk further damage."

Jeremiah's expression remained firm. "Orders are orders, Dr. Shaw. Without an official statement from Dr. Weiss, we are not authorized to shut down the collider."

Meanwhile, Thomas and Nadia continued their heated debate. Thomas' eyes sparkled with a fervent passion, the same which the two women had witnessed on the day the LHC had come to life. "This experiment is incredible! It's like something out of a movie. We're on the brink of a groundbreaking discovery!"

Nadia, clearly exasperated, snorted, "And in every one of those movies, humanity suffers for the first half! Do you really want to see that play out here in real life?"

Thomas faltered, clearly torn by her words. "But the potential for discovery-"

"Is outweighed by the potential for disaster!" Nadia shot back, her voice rising. "We've already seen the anomalies spread. Continuing this is reckless and dangerous." She added, hands resting on her hips as she leaned up to glare at the rangy young man. "Face it; if this goes out of hand, we'd be the first ones to die."

Evelyn took a step toward Jeremiah, her voice firm and unyielding. "The anomalies are spreading. We're risking not just the success of the experiment but the safety of the entire world. We must shut it down. Now!"

Jeremiah's face was set like stone. "I understand your concerns, Dr. Shaw, but unless you can produce an official statement from Dr.

Weiss countermanding his previous orders, I will not shut down the collider."

Evelyn's heart sank. She knew convincing Dr. Weiss to issue such a statement would be nearly impossible. He was determined to see the experiment through, regardless of the consequences. She glanced at Nadia, whose eyes reflected the same grim understanding.

"Jeremy," Evelyn said, trying to appeal to the fact the two had worked closely over the past decade or so. "You're making a grave mistake; the risks are too great."

Jeremiah's eyes softened for a fraction, but for the most part, he remained unmoved. "Without official clearance from Dr. Weiss, my hands are tied, *Dr. Shaw.*" He emphasized the usage of formalities in a way that felt like an intentional jab at something only the two were aware of. "We will proceed as ordered."

The room fell into a tense silence. Thomas and Nadia's argument ceased, both of them looking toward Evelyn, waiting for her next move. She knew they were right, but without Jeremiah's cooperation, her hands were tied as well.

Evelyn took a deep breath, trying to quell the disappointment bubbling inside her. "Very well, *Jeremiah.* I'll get the statement. But know this: every second we delay increases the risk. If we can't shut it down soon, the consequences will be on all of us."

Jeremiah's face remained inscrutable; his arms still crossed over his chest. "Understood, Dr. Shaw."

As she turned to leave, Evelyn felt a heavy weight settle on her shoulders. The fight to shut down the collider was far from over, and she would need to confront Dr. Weiss directly. She was determined to prevent further breaches and protect the world from the dangerous ambitions of their experiment, even if it meant challenging her superiors and risking her career. She exited the control room, her mind racing with the challenges ahead. The anomalies were a dire warning, and she was resolved to do whatever it took to fix the breaches and restore balance to their world. The battle had only just begun, and she would not back down.

Dr. Evelyn Shaw stood on the balcony, gazing out over the expansive snowy plains that stretched into the horizon. The bitter cold of the North Dakota winter surrounded her, but her thoughts were consumed by the escalating crisis within the research facility. The decision to continue the experiment despite the growing anomalies gnawed at her conscience, knowing the potential risks to humanity.

Lost in her contemplation, she was startled by the sound of approaching footsteps on the snow-covered balcony. Nadia, her face serious and determined, joined Evelyn at the railing. She fiddled nervously with her phone before finally speaking up.

"Doctor, if you're truly determined to stop this, we might need outside help. Someone who isn't bound by the same contracts and associations as we are," Nadia began, her voice low but resolute.

Evelyn turned to her, her expression curious yet cautious. "What do you mean?"

Nadia met her gaze squarely. "We could try to expose this operation to the public. Create enough outrage that the government has no choice but to shut it down or at least postpone further experiments."

Evelyn nodded slowly, considering the implications. "It's a risky move, Nadia. We would be putting everything on the line."

"I know," she replied earnestly. "But if we don't do something, who knows what could happen? The anomalies are already spreading, and we're running out of time."

Evelyn sighed, her breath forming a mist in the cold air. "Do you have someone in mind? Someone who could help us?"

Nadia hesitated, her gaze distant for a moment. "I... I have a family member," she began carefully. "A journalist. They've been investigating similar incidents and might have the connections to bring this to light."

Evelyn raised an eyebrow, intrigued. "Do you trust them?"

Nadia nodded firmly. "Yes, I do. They've always been driven by a sense of justice. If anyone can help us expose what's happening here, it's them."

Evelyn considered Nadia's words for a moment, weighing the risks and the potential benefits. They needed a voice outside of their controlled environment, someone who could speak freely without fear of repercussions.

"Alright," Evelyn said finally, her voice steady with resolve. "Let's reach out to your contact. We'll need solid evidence, something that will convince them to investigate further."

Nadia nodded in agreement. "I'll contact them tonight. We'll have to be careful, but if we play our cards right, we might just have a chance."

As they stood side by side, facing the daunting challenges ahead, Evelyn felt a sense of relief knowing she wasn't alone in this fight. Together with Nadia and the journalist, they could shine a light on the dangers they had unleashed and, hopefully, force those responsible to take action.

"Thank you, Nadia," Evelyn said sincerely, a small smile tugging at her lips. "For believing in what's right and for standing with me."

Nadia returned her smile, determination shining in her eyes. "We're in this together, Dr. Shaw. Whatever happens, we'll face it together."

With renewed purpose, Evelyn and Nadia turned their attention back to the research facility behind them. The looming structure held the key to their future—and potentially the future of the world. They were ready to challenge the status quo, no matter the cost, for the sake of truth and the safety of humanity.

* * *

Marcus Flynn stepped out of the airport terminal into the crisp Fargo air, his breath forming mist in front of him. Adjusting the strap of his bag over his shoulder, he scanned the bustling crowd for any sign of Nadia. She had promised to meet him here and introduce him to Dr. Evelyn Shaw, someone who could help unravel the secrets of the LHC.

The airport buzzed with activity—travelers rushing by, announcements echoing through the hall. Marcus' anticipation mingled with apprehension. He had spoken briefly with Nadia, and her assurances about Dr. Shaw's brilliance, influence, and willingness to meet him had piqued his curiosity.

Spotting her amidst the throng, he recognized Nadia's slender figure, her dusky complexion standing out among the crowd. Her long, unruly curls framed her face, and she wore a distinct dress-coat gifted to her by Marcus' wife—an event he had specifically been uninvited from by her father, his brother-in-law.

"Mornin', lass," Marcus greeted warmly as he approached her. "Good to see you."

Nadia smiled warmly. "Of course, Uncle. I'm glad you're here. Dr. Shaw is waiting. Follow me."

Steering through the bustling terminal, she led him to a quieter area near the airport cafe where Dr. Evelyn Shaw stood waiting. Dr. Shaw, with her composed demeanor and intelligent gaze, exuded an air of authority tempered by a hint of concern.

"Uncle Mark," Nadia introduced him, her voice respectful. "This is Dr. Evelyn Shaw. She's the physicist I mentioned, eager to discuss your inquiries about the LHC."

Dr. Shaw extended her hand, which Marcus shook firmly. "Good to meet you, Mr. Flynn," she greeted, her voice carrying a weight of purpose. "Nadia has spoken highly of your interest in uncovering the truth. Shall we find a quieter spot to talk?"

They moved to a nearby seating area, away from the bustling crowds. Dr. Shaw wasted no time in getting down to business.

"She's mentioned you have questions about the LHC," Dr. Shaw began, her tone measured but attentive. "What specifically are you hoping to find?"

Marcus leaned forward, his gaze meeting Dr. Shaw's with determination. "I need to understand what's really going on there. There have been anomalies and strange occurrences tied to their experiments. I want to expose the truth."

Dr. Shaw nodded thoughtfully. "It won't be easy. The operations at the LHC are tightly controlled and veiled in secrecy. But with your resolve, we might have a chance."

The three gathered in a secluded area near the airport cafe. The atmosphere was charged with anticipation as they discussed their shared suspicions and the looming mysteries surrounding the LHC.

"So, Marcus," Dr. Shaw began, her tone rigid yet tinged with curiosity. "Can you elaborate on what you've uncovered so far?"

Marcus shifted in his seat, his mind racing with fragments of information and half-formed theories. "I've been tracking reports of strange phenomena—unexplained power surges, disruptions in local electromagnetic fields, even sightings of unusual lights and sounds near the facility. There's definitely something significant happening."

"How are you certain that it links to the LHC?" Dr. Shaw asked, raising a skeptical eyebrow at Marcus.

He, looking as poker-faced as ever, leaned back in his seat. "How are you certain that it's not?" He inquired smugly.

She clicked her tongue, shaking her head. "I never said it didn't; I was asking about your sources," she elaborated.

He shook his head, taking out a cigarette from his jacket's pocket and lighting it up with a zippo lighter. "I'm here to uncover your secrets, not give you a tour of my work. Where I get my information is none of your concern, got it?"

Nadia, sensing the tension, quietly looked down at her phone, pretending to type on it.

Dr. Shaw glanced over at her, then at the man seated opposite to her. She took a deep breath and decided to explain herself a bit better. "I am asking because we might need their help too; this isn't a one-man mission, Mr. Flynn."

A plume of smoke emitted from his mouth as he narrowed his eyes at her, deciding on how much he trusted her. Realizing that he'd need to at least appeal to her sense of trust before he could get into the nitty-gritty of this mess.

"A few different sources, for now, this hacker called Phoenix on the Dark Web. That's the guy that sent me the files about your experiments-"

Nadia's head shot up, sighing. "I knew that'd happen sooner or later; no matter what they do, someone can always pick their locks from the outside."

Dr. Shaw listened intently, her brow furrowing with concern. "If what you're saying is true, Mr. Flynn, we could be dealing with serious consequences. The LHC's experiments are meant to push the boundaries of physics, but if they're inadvertently causing dimensional disruptions..."

Marcus finished her thought, his voice grave. "It could threaten the fabric of reality itself."

Silence hung heavy in the air as they processed the implications of their conversation. The gravity of their task weighed on them, but it only strengthened their resolve.

"We need to investigate this further," Dr. Shaw asserted, her gaze determined. "Nadia, can you access any internal documents or schedules that might shed light on their recent experiments?"

Nadia nodded thoughtfully. "I can try. I have access to some restricted areas and documents, but I'll need to be cautious. Maybe Dr. Petrova could help out?"

Marcus leaned forward, his eyes meeting Dr. Shaw's with an unbridled intensity. " If we can build a compelling case, we might force them to reveal what they're really doing."

Dr. Shaw nodded in agreement. "We'll need solid evidence to confront them effectively."

Nadia looked between them, a sense of determination in her eyes. "I'll start gathering what I can discreetly. If we find anything significant, we'll reconvene and strategize our next move."

With their plan outlined, they spent the next hour discussing logistics—communication protocols, safe meeting locations, and contingency plans in case their investigations attracted unwanted attention. As they prepared to depart, Dr. Shaw stood, her expression resolute. "Thank you both for coming forward with this. Together, we have a chance to uncover the truth and protect humanity from potential catastrophe."

They exchanged contact information and parted ways, each committed to their respective roles in unraveling the mysteries of the LHC.

Colonel John Harrows sat in his secluded cabin, the warmth of a crackling fire doing little to alleviate the cold that had settled deep into his bones. The North Dakota mountains were unforgiving, their snow-covered peaks casting long shadows as the sun dipped below the horizon. Outside, a biting wind howled through the trees, but inside, the cabin was a sanctuary of solitude and quiet reflection.

Max, his loyal German Shepherd, lay curled up on the bed, a thick blanket draped over him to stave off the chill. His ears twitched occasionally, reacting to the creaks and groans of the wooden structure, but he remained relaxed, trusting in the safety of his master's presence.

Colonel Harrows, known as "Reaper" for his strategic prowess and unyielding resolve, leaned back in his chair, staring into the dancing flames. The dim light cast shadows on his weathered face, highlighting the lines etched by years of service and countless missions undertaken in the name of duty and country.

The past few days had been a whirlwind of cryptic messages and late-night exchanges with an elusive virtual vigilante known only as Phoenix. Harrows' computer screen glowed faintly in the corner, displaying the latest correspondence—a string of encrypted emails and coordinates that hinted at the location of a Cabal base, a clandestine organization with nefarious motives.

"Where will this lead me?" he mused aloud, his voice a gravelly whisper barely audible over the crackling fire. "Is it honor that drives me or something else?"

His mind wandered to the faces of the soldiers he had led, the comrades he had lost. The principles of duty and honor that had guided him through countless battles now felt like fragile lifelines in a world increasingly blurred by deceit and conspiracy. The Cabal, a cult with a terrifying grip on those desperate for purpose, posed a threat that could not be ignored.

Phoenix had been his unexpected ally in this new, covert war. Their communication had been sparse but precise, each message laden with veiled warnings and crucial information. Harrows had managed to piece together a rough location of the Cabal's base, hidden deep within the sprawling wilderness of North Dakota. But the exact coordinates remained elusive, and time was running out.

Max shifted on the bed, letting out a soft, contented sigh, and Harrows glanced over, a faint smile tugging at his lips. "You're the only one who doesn't ask questions," he said softly, his hand absently reaching for the old, leather-bound notebook on the table beside him.

Inside, scribbled notes and hastily drawn maps documented his progress, a testament to his tireless pursuit of justice. The computer screen flickered, drawing his attention back to the present. Another message from Phoenix had arrived, the subject line a stark reminder of the urgency of their mission:

Coordinates Enclosed - Act Fast

Harrows leaned forward, his fingers flying over the keyboard as he decrypted the message. The screen displayed a set of coordinates and a terse message:

This is it. Be prepared for anything. Trust no one.

He memorized the coordinates, feeling a surge of adrenaline that momentarily banished the weariness from his bones. The location was not far from his cabin, hidden in the rugged terrain that had served as his refuge. He closed the laptop, the weight of the next steps settling heavily on his shoulders.

Max lifted his head, sensing the shift in his master's demeanor. Harrows reached over, scratching behind the dog's ears, his mind already strategizing the next move. "It's time, old friend," he murmured. "We have a mission."

Rising from his chair, he crossed the room to a sturdy wooden chest, lifting the lid to reveal an array of weapons and survival gear. He methodically selected his equipment, checking each piece with the precision of a man who had spent a lifetime preparing for the unknown.

As he strapped on his gear, Harrows paused by the window, peering out into the darkening landscape. The mountains loomed, silent witnesses to the unfolding drama. The Cabal's stronghold was out there, hidden and waiting, and he would find it and dismantle it piece by piece if necessary.

With one last look around the cabin, Harrows turned to Max, who was now fully alert, ready for whatever lay ahead. "Let's go, Max. We have work to do."

Together, they stepped into the frigid night, the cabin's warmth receding behind them as they ventured into the unforgiving wilderness. Harrows' mind was focused, his resolve unshaken. The Cabal's secrets would be uncovered, and justice, though elusive, would be served.

The hunt had begun.

* * *

Zara Akhtar sat on the worn wooden bench of a bus stop in Manchester, her hood pulled tightly over her head to shield herself from the relentless drizzle. The day was as grey and dreary as her mood, the sky a uniform sheet of cloud that seemed to press down on the city. Raindrops spattered the pavement, creating tiny rivers that trickled into the gutter.

She tried to focus on mundane things—her mother's homemade biryani, the comforting aroma still lingering in her small flat after her mother's visit from Leeds. Her mother had been worried about her, urging her to take a break, to find a steady job, to meet someone nice. Zara sighed, the memory both warm and bittersweet.

Eesah's unanswered text also lingered in her thoughts. The guy from the local garage, with his easy smile and grease-streaked hands, had seemed genuinely interested in her. They had chatted a few times, and she had even considered asking him out for coffee. But she had never mustered the courage, always feeling like her world of codes and conspiracies was too alien for someone like him.

But no matter how hard she tried, her mind always drifted back to her brother Faisal. He had been her rock, her mentor in the labyrinthine world of hacking and digital espionage. His loss was a wound that had never truly healed, and every line of code, every script she wrote, felt like a tribute to his memory.

She was lost in thought, envisioning the intricate layers of a particularly challenging photonic script, when her phone buzzed with a new message. The notification was from an unknown number, and she hesitated for a moment before opening it.

The message was stark, its simplicity chilling:

We can help you. The Cabal will be no more.

Zara's heart skipped a beat, a mixture of fear and excitement flooding her veins. The Cabal. She had been tracking them for months, piecing together fragments of data and whispers on the dark web. They were more than just a cult; they were a shadowy organization with fingers in every pie, from political manipulation to illegal technological advancements.

She looked around; the rain-slicked streets were almost deserted save for a few huddled figures under umbrellas. She knew the message was no accident. Whoever had sent it knew her, had tracked her, singled her out, knew her work, and most importantly, knew her desire to dismantle the Cabal.

***

The dim lighting in Nadia's tiny one-bedroom apartment cast a soft glow over the modest furnishings. The space was cozy, though a bit cluttered, with books and notes strewn across a small dining table. The walls were adorned with a few framed photos, mostly of family gatherings and university graduations, giving the place a personal touch.

Nadia stood by her dresser, brushing her damp hair. The rhythmic strokes of the brush through her thick, curly locks were almost meditative, a simple act that grounded her in the midst of the chaos swirling around them. She wore a faded blue robe, the soft fabric clinging to her slender frame as she moved with practiced ease in the cramped space.

Marcus sat on the edge of Nadia's bed, his eyes glued to the screen of his phone. The bed was neatly made, a contrast to the rest of the apartment, with a simple white duvet and a few plump pillows. His fingers moved rapidly across the keypad as he typed, pausing occasionally to consider his next message. The faint tapping was the only sound in the room, blending with the quiet hum of the city outside.

He had managed to enlist the help of Shade, who had deciphered the codes from the private chatroom hosted by Phoenix, leading Marcus to over fifteen different contacts. Each one was a potential key to finding the identity of this individual and contacting them personally.

"I've sent messages to all of them," Marcus said, his voice tinged with a mixture of anticipation and exhaustion. "Now, we wait."

Nadia turned to face him, her hair falling in loose waves around her shoulders. She set the brush down and moved to the small kitchenette, the clinking of mugs and the hiss of the kettle indicating her intention to make tea.

"You're welcome to crash on the sofa if you need to," she offered, her voice warm and inviting despite the fatigue that lingered in her eyes. "It's not much, but it's better than nothing."

Marcus looked up, a grateful smile softening his usually stern features. "Thanks, Nadia. I appreciate it."

As she busied herself with the tea, Marcus took the opportunity to probe further into the workings of the LHC. "Tell me more about the people there," he said, leaning back against the wall. "Who's who in this madhouse?"

Nadia sighed, setting two steaming mugs on the small coffee table before sitting down on the edge of a chair across from Marcus.

She took a sip of her tea, the warmth seeping into her hands as she gathered her thoughts.

"Well, there's Jeremiah," she began. "He's a veteran mechanic and technician. Reliable, experienced, but also very stubborn. He's the kind of guy who's seen it all and isn't easily swayed by anything."

"Sounds like the type who'd be hard to convince to stop a project," Marcus noted. "Or to talk too much about it."

"Exactly," Nadia agreed, nodding. "Then there's Dr. Anton Weiss, the head of the entire operation. He's...complicated. Brilliant, but with a serious lack of empathy. He's driven by the science, the potential discoveries, and he doesn't really care about the risks involved."

Marcus frowned. "And he's the one pushing for the continuation of these experiments?"

"Yes," Nadia confirmed. "Weiss is the driving force. He's not easy to argue with, especially since he holds so much authority. But he's not the only one involved. There's Dr. Anya Petrova, his assistant. She's a good person, really, but she's very much under Weiss' influence. I think she believes in the potential of their work, even if it means turning a blind eye to the dangers."

"And the kiwi?" Marcus asked, recalling her earlier mention of the excitable technician.

"Thomas is like a kid in a candy store," she said, a faint smile tugging at her lips. "He's overly excited about the whole thing and sees it as a grand adventure. He doesn't really grasp the potential consequences. For him, it's like something out of a sci-fi movie."

Marcus nodded, absorbing the information. "Sounds like a mixed bag of characters. It's going to be a challenge getting through to any of them, especially if Weiss is as influential as you say."

Nadia sighed again, her shoulders slumping slightly. "It is. But we can't give up. Dr. Shaw says that there's too much at stake, and I agree with her."

Marcus set his phone aside, reaching for his mug. The warmth of the tea was a welcome comfort in the chilly apartment. "We'll figure it out, lass. One step at a time. And maybe these contacts will lead us to something useful."

Nadia looked at him, a flicker of hope in her eyes. "I hope so. For all our sakes."

The room fell into a companionable silence, the weight of their shared burden hanging in the air. Outside, the city lights flickered, casting a soft glow through the curtains. Despite the uncertainty of the path ahead, there was a sense of determination between them — a silent agreement to see this through, no matter the cost.

Chapter 3: The Gathering

Zara stood in the airport security line, an odd sense of unease mingling with the routine annoyances of travel. The bustling terminal was filled with the sounds of announcements, the rolling of luggage wheels, and the murmurs of travelers. She shifted her weight from one foot to the other, clutching her worn backpack tightly.

The past few days had been a whirlwind. The mysterious text message had appeared out of nowhere, disrupting her already turbulent thoughts. The sender claimed to have vital information about the anomalies plaguing the world and their connection to the LHC—a particle collider she had only heard about in conspiracy theories and half-whispered rumors on the dark web. But she had forwarded whatever she had found to an unknown individual using the alias 'BigRedStud' during an online discussion some week or so ago. Her mind drifted back to the first message:

We can help you. The Cabal will be no more.

She had dismissed it initially, thinking it was just another crackpot trying to lure her into a trap. But the subsequent messages had been different. They were precise, detailed, and filled with information only someone on the inside could know. She had verified some of the data herself, cross-referencing with her own sources and findings. The coordinates she had been given were situated in North Dakota, a place she never thought she would have any reason to visit.

The line shuffled forward. She handed her passport and boarding pass to the security officer, who barely glanced at her before waving her through. Placing her backpack on the conveyor belt, she stepped through the metal detector, her heart pounding a little harder than usual.

As she waited for her belongings to emerge from the X-ray machine, her thoughts returned to the messages. The mysterious contact had revealed details about the LHC's real purpose—something far more sinister than what the public was told. According to the messages, the collider was not just a particle physics experiment; it was a portal to other dimensions. The anomalies—strange lights, sonic booms, and disruptions in reality—were all symptoms of this tampering with the fabric of the universe.

Bring your wits intact, the last message had advised. *It's not for the faint of heart.*

She had spent years digging into secrets, exposing corruption, and hacking into systems that were supposedly impenetrable. But this felt different. The stakes were higher, the risks more personal. She thought of her brother for an uncountable time. She realized this might be her chance to honor his memory. It was due to that desire that she had given username Reaper the coordinates to the Cabal. He might've been skilled, but he wasn't tech-savvy, she thought. She was aware of retired military officer John Harrows being Reaper but decided that if he were on the right side, his being unable to conceal his identity didn't matter much.

When her backpack finally appeared, she grabbed it, slinging it over her shoulder. She moved towards the gate, her mind racing with possibilities and fears. Who was this contact? Why had they chosen her? And what exactly would she find in North Dakota?

She found a seat near the gate, her fingers tapping nervously on her phone. Opening the encrypted messaging app, she reread the messages, looking for any clues she might have missed. The sender's identity was still a mystery, hidden behind layers of digital obfuscation. All she knew was that this person had a deep understanding of the situation and seemed to be on her side.

So, that made almost three of them? Phoenix, Reaper, and whoever this guy was.

As the boarding call echoed through the terminal, Zara stood up, her resolve hardening. She was no stranger to danger, and if this was as important as it seemed, she couldn't turn back now. She would follow the coordinates, meet whoever was behind the messages, and uncover the truth about the LHC, the anomalies, and what the Cabal had to do with it all. For Faisal, for herself, and unbeknownst to her, for the world teetering on the brink of a new reality.

***

John Harrows gripped the steering wheel of the worn-out rental car, his knuckles white against the cracked leather. The road ahead stretched out in an endless ribbon of asphalt, disappearing into the horizon. The landscape was barren, the cold North Dakota air biting even through the closed windows. The old car's heater struggled to keep the chill at bay, and the engine hummed with a tired persistence.

Max, his loyal German Shepherd, lay curled up on the passenger seat, a blanket draped over him. The dog's ears occasionally twitched at the sound of the tires on the rough road, but he remained mostly still, sensing his master's focus and determination.

Harrows glanced at the GPS on his phone, the coordinates he had received from Phoenix glowing ominously on the screen. Phoenix—a name that had become synonymous with secret information and covert assistance. They had been exchanging information for months now, each tip more crucial than the last. Harrows had come to rely on these communications, each one guiding him deeper into the mystery of the LHC and its dark implications.

The latest coordinates pointed to a location just outside Fargo, and Phoenix's message had been clear:

The LHC project is somewhere off Fargo. The same coordinates that were previously provided for the Cabal's possible headquarters. You know what that means.

He knew that LHC was trouble and suspected the Cabal's involvement, but this had just turned that suspicion into belief. Harrows' mind raced as he drove, replaying the past few days in his head. The tip had been unexpected, and the connection between the LHC and the Cabal—a shadowy cult with ties to bizarre scientific endeavors and esoteric practices—had sent chills down his spine.

He remembered the days he had spent working on providing military-level security to the transportation of the LHC machinery back when it was just another classified project. As the car bumped over a pothole, Harrows tightened his grip on the wheel. Max lifted his head, sensing his master's tension, and gave a low, reassuring whine.

"It's okay, buddy," Harrows murmured, reaching over to pat the dog's head. "We're almost there."

He couldn't shake the feeling that he was being watched, that every move he made was under scrutiny. The landscape around him was desolate, offering no cover, but he knew better than to underestimate his enemies. The Cabal was known for their reach and their ruthlessness, and now it seemed they were entangled with the LHC in ways he had yet to fully understand.

The miles slipped by, the sun dipping lower in the sky, casting long shadows across the road. Harrows' thoughts turned to Phoenix. He had never met the enigmatic figure, but their interactions had been invaluable. Whoever Phoenix was, they had a deep understanding of the situation and a willingness to share critical information. He had learned to trust those tips, even as he questioned the motives behind them.

Finally, the GPS indicated that he was approaching the coordinates. The road narrowed, flanked by dense woods and open fields, the isolation palpable. Harrows slowed the car, scanning the area for any signs of life. The coordinates pointed to a seemingly unremarkable patch of land, but he knew better than to take things at face value. He pulled the car to a stop, the engine ticking as it cooled. Max jumped down from the seat, shaking off the blanket and stretching his legs. Harrows stepped out, the cold air hitting him like a slap. He zipped up his jacket and took a deep breath, his eyes narrowing as he surveyed the area.

Phoenix's last message echoed in his mind:

Bring your wits intact. It's not for the faint of heart.

He had faced many challenges in his life, but this felt like the most critical yet. The intersection of science and mysticism, the LHC and the Cabal—he was standing at the nexus of something monumental. He reached back into the car, pulling out a duffel bag filled with supplies—maps, tools, and a few weapons, just in case. He couldn't afford to be unprepared. As he slung the bag over his shoulder, Max at his side, Harrows set off towards the coordinates, hoping that he hadn't arrived too late.

* * *

Nadia moved swiftly through the sterile hallways of the research facility, her heels clicking sharply against the polished floor. Marcus followed close behind, taking in on the architecture and the occasional worker walking past. The fluorescent lights cast a clinical glow, making the surroundings feel both modern and slightly unnerving. His niece's demeanor was composed, but he could sense the underlying tension in her movements.

"So, *sir*," Nadia said loudly, her voice echoing slightly in the empty corridor, "as a journalist, you must be fascinated by the cutting-edge research we're conducting here."

Marcus nodded, playing along. "*Absolutely.* It's not every day you get to see the forefront of scientific advancement. Could you tell me more about the specific projects you're working on?"

She glanced over her shoulder, giving him a knowing look before turning back to face forward. "Of course, but let's keep moving. There's so much to show you."

They rounded a corner, and Nadia nearly collided with Thomas, the ever-enthusiastic gangly technician. His curly brown hair hadn't been combed or gelled as he looked up from his clipboard and down at her with wide, surprised eyes.

"Oh, I didn't see yo-huh?" Thomas paused mid-sentence when his gaze shifted to Marcus. "Who's, uh, who's this?"

Nadia forced a smile, trying to maintain an air of casual confidence. "Thomas, this is Mr. Ben Gunn. He's a journalist here to write a piece on our facility. I've cleared it with Dr. Shaw."

Thomas' eyebrows knitted together in confusion. "I didn't get a memo about this. Are you sure it's okay for him to be here?"

Marcus, sensing the need to bolster Nadia's story, stepped forward with a friendly smile and held up a ridiculously well-made fake ID. "Don't worry, man. I'm just here to observe and report on the amazing work you all are doing, like the work on Black Holes and all that. It'll be great publicity for the facility."

Thomas hesitated, glancing between Nadia and Marcus. "I suppose... but there are protocols. We can't just let anyone wander around, especially near the more sensitive areas."

Nadia nodded, trying to maintain her composure. "Absolutely. We're just giving him a general tour. Nothing too specific."

Thomas' eyes narrowed slightly, still unsure. "Alright, but make sure he doesn't go anywhere he's not supposed to, as it could be dangerous."

Nadia breathed a sigh of relief. "Of course. Thanks."

As Thomas walked away, still casting suspicious glances over his shoulder, Nadia motioned for Marcus to follow her down another hallway. They moved quickly; the urgency of their mission was clear.

Once they were out of earshot, Marcus leaned in and whispered, "Ben Gunn?" he chuckled, looking slightly amused.

She rolled her eyes, checking to see if the passcode pad was active or not. "I'm not good with names."

"That was close. How are we going to get past the more secure areas?" he inquired.

Luckily for them, the access pad was active, and she put in the assigned combination, causing the doors to slide to their sides for them to enter through.

"Like this," she muttered, leading the way.

The inside was comprised of white tiles, florescent lights, and meticulously arranged machinery. Glass capsules, some with fluids while others with odd-looking rocks of sorts, floated within them. Some large pods with thick pipelines and wires attached to them were laid out professionally all over the enormous room. Nadia didn't waste any time. Instead, she pushed open a heavy door to the underground chamber. The sound of its creaking hinges echoing ominously in the cavernous space beyond. They climbed down the staircase until reaching what could only be described as a metallic wall.

This one had an eye scanner placed beside it, one that she used to unlock the gateway. The 'wall' whirred as its panels slid in different directions, allowing them to enter. She stepped aside, allowing Marcus to go in first. As he crossed the threshold, his breath caught in his throat at the sight before him.

The Large Hadron Collider (LHC) stretched out in a colossal ring, its immense structure snaking through the subterranean chamber like a gargantuan, coiled serpent. The sheer scale of the machine was overwhelming, dwarfing everything around it. Massive superconducting magnets lined the collider's circumference, their sleek, metallic surfaces gleaming under the harsh fluorescent lights that illuminated the chamber.

The walls of the cavern were lined with an array of control panels, monitors, and cables, all humming with a low, constant buzz of energy. The air was cool and dry, carrying a faint smell of ozone and machinery. The floor beneath their feet was a polished, industrial-grade metal, reflecting the cold, sterile environment.

He took a few tentative steps forward, his eyes wide as he absorbed the details of the scene. He felt a mix of awe and trepidation, aware that he was standing in the presence of one of humanity's greatest technological achievements—and possibly its most dangerous.

"It's... incredible," he whispered, his voice barely audible over the ambient noise of the chamber.

Nadia nodded with a mix of pride and concern. "Yes, it is; Dr. Shaw calls it the living proof of *Exodia*. But it's also why we're here; the power and potential of this machine are beyond anything most people can imagine."

They moved closer to the collider, the sound of their footsteps swallowed by the vastness of the space. Marcus could see the intricate network of wires and sensors attached to the machine, each one playing a crucial role in its operation. The collider's inner workings were a maze of high-tech components, a testament to the cutting-edge science and engineering that had gone into its creation.

As they approached the central control station, Marcus noticed a large, transparent viewport that allowed a clear view of the collider's core. He peered through it, marveling at the sight of the particle beam channels—thin, perfectly aligned tubes through which particles would be accelerated to near-light speeds before colliding with unimaginable force.

"This is where it all happens," Nadia said, her voice tinged with a hint of reverence. "The collisions that take place here are capable of recreating conditions similar to those just after the Big Bang. The potential for discovery is immense... but so are the risks."

Marcus nodded, his mind racing with thoughts of the anomalies and disruptions he had been investigating. "And this is where the dimensional breaches occurred?"

Nadia's expression darkened. "The first one, yes. Last week's experiment went beyond what anyone anticipated. The first breach that was detected was... unprecedented."

Marcus felt the gears in his head turn as he stared at the collider. The magnitude of their task was daunting, and he knew that uncovering the truth was paramount. However, being there, in its presence, he couldn't deny that something about the whole situation felt...odd. His niece had been so secretive about this, but now both she and her superior were ready to have him walk into this mess.

"I'm your scapegoat, aren't I, lass?" he asked, half amused.

Her eyes lowered at his words, making it obvious that he was correct. "It's not like that. We, you know, we signed a contract and whatnot. We'd be convicted of war crime if we did anything to break that contract." Even when she tried to explain herself, she could feel that those words held less to no weight. He was right. They were using him not only because of his capabilities but because they knew he needed something like this, and they needed someone to take the fall for them.

He shook his head, narrowing his eyes at the mechanical giant in front of them. "I don't think just public outrage would be enough for this. This needs to be taken apart."

Nadia nodded, her eyes still downcast from a mixture of embarrassment and guilt. "I'm aware, but we'd need the engineers to do that."

Understanding her grievance, he simply sighed. "A'right, least get to work and show us how it's working. Maybe there's a weakness in the system we can use." Then, turning around to the direction they'd come from, he groaned. "Where the bloody hell is that Doctor of yours?"

"Dr. Shaw is probably trying to convince other members of the teams to abandon ship. After all, we need all the help we can get."

Together, they began to examine the control panels and data readouts, searching for any clues that might explain the anomalies in-depth and the true extent of the LHC's capabilities. The stakes were getting higher by the second, but they were determined to uncover the secrets hidden within this massive machine, no matter the cost.

* * *

John Harrow's breath formed misty clouds in the frigid air as he moved stealthily through the snow-covered terrain. The cold made his bones ache, but he ignored it, his focus on the distant silhouette of the research facility. The dim light of the pre-dawn sky cast long shadows, providing him with just enough cover to remain concealed.

His faithful German Shepherd, Max, sat obediently in the front seat of the worn-out rental car, parked strategically off the road and partially hidden by a grove of bare trees. He had made sure to leave the car door ajar so Max could come and go as he pleased, ensuring he had access to the food and water supplies stashed in the back seat. Max, trained for such situations, seemed to understand the gravity of the command to stay put, his intelligent eyes tracking John's movements as he prepared to leave.

"Stay here, buddy. I'll be back soon," John whispered, giving Max a reassuring pat on the head. The dog responded with a quiet, obedient whine, settling down in the seat. Seeing that, John slipped on a lab coat he had brought, hoping to blend in with the crowd inside.

With one last glance at Max, John turned and set off towards the facility, his movements silent and calculated. The snowy landscape muffled his footsteps, and the early morning stillness was only broken by the occasional rustle of wind through the trees. He kept low, using the natural cover provided by the undulating terrain to his advantage. As he neared the research facility, the structure loomed larger; its sleek, modern lines looked strange against the natural backdrop. He paused for a moment, scanning the perimeter for any signs of patrols or surveillance cameras. The building appeared deceptively quiet, but he knew better than to trust appearances. He pulled out his phone, checking the passcodes that Phoenix had encrypted and sent him. Each code was a potential key to unlocking the facility's defenses.

There were definitely automated guards around. Meaning that if there were army personnel, it was within the inner walls while the outermost was guarded by vigilant machinery. John approached a side entrance, one that seemed less fortified than the main gates. He crouched near the door, taking a deep breath to steady his nerves. His fingers moved swiftly, entering the first of the passcodes into the security panel beside the door. The screen blinked, processing the input before displaying a green light and an audible click as the lock disengaged.

He slipped inside, the door closing softly behind him. The interior was just as barren and high-tech as he had expected, the walls lined with sleek, white panels and the floor a polished, reflective surface. He moved cautiously, his senses heightened, listening for any sound that might indicate someone approaching. John navigated through a series of corridors, each turn bringing him closer to his objective. The layout of the facility matched the schematics of the map he had memorized, allowing him to move with a certain degree of confidence. He reached another security checkpoint, this one requiring a more complex code. Again, he referred to Phoenix's encrypted message, entering the sequence with precision. The door slid open, granting him access to the inner sections of the facility.

The further he went, the more he felt the weight of the secrets hidden within these walls. He knew that the LHC was at the heart of something much bigger than anyone had anticipated, something that threatened the very fabric of reality. His military training kept him focused, every step bringing him closer to uncovering the truth. As he rounded a final corner, the distant hum of machinery grew louder. He knew he was nearing the chamber where the collider was housed.

He paused, taking a moment to assess his surroundings and plan his next move. The facility might have appeared deserted, but he couldn't afford to let his guard down.

The fact that the place was *this* quiet grated on his nerves. Through this whole time, he had seen maybe three to four people walk there. It seemed unnatural, to say the least.

"Where the hell is everyone?" he mumbled to himself.

Soon enough, he found himself standing at yet another security door, the blue glow of the control panel illuminating his face. He reached into his pocket and pulled out his phone, ready to input the final passcode Phoenix had sent him. As he began to punch in the numbers, his phone vibrated with an incoming message.

He glanced at the screen. It was from an unknown number, but he had a feeling it was Phoenix since they had the habit of never messaging from the same number twice.

>Phoenix

Collider spotted?

John's fingers hovered over the keys as he considered how to respond. He quickly typed a brief reply: *Not yet, just about to enter the inner chamber.*

He sent the message and turned back to the panel, finishing the sequence of numbers. The screen blinked, processing the input. Suddenly, the silence was shattered by a blaring alarm, red lights flashing throughout the corridor.

"Oh, fuck," he muttered under his breath, realizing the code was incorrect.

The alarm's shrill sound echoed off the walls, making it impossible to think clearly. He knew he had only seconds to act before security would converge on his location. Scanning the corridor, he looked for any possible escape route or hiding place. John's pulse quickened. He looked around, spotting a maintenance closet a few meters away. He sprinted towards it, the alarm still blaring in his ears. He reached the door, yanked it open, and slipped inside just as he heard the pounding of footsteps approaching.

Inside the cramped closet, he closed the door quietly, pressing his back against the wall. He listened intently, trying to gauge the situation outside. The footsteps grew louder, then stopped just outside his hiding spot. He held his breath, straining to hear any conversation or movement.

"What's going on?" a voice demanded, authoritative and sharp.

"Someone's breached this section," another voice replied. "We need to search the area. Check every room."

John's heart pounded as he heard the sound of doors being opened and checked one by one. He knew it was only a matter of time before they reached his hiding spot. He typed on his phone, praying that his ally would have his back.

>*Reapers*

Password 3 incorrect. I might be discovered.

Seconds felt like hours as the search continued. He readied himself, anticipating the worst. Getting caught wasn't something he needed right now, given how he was finally in the lion's den.

Finally, his phone buzzed again with the new code. He quickly memorized it, knowing he had only one shot. The footsteps grew fainter as the search team moved further down the corridor. Taking a deep breath, he slowly opened the closet door, peeking out to ensure the coast was clear.

He stepped out, moving quickly back to the security panel. With the new code fresh in his mind, he entered the sequence with swift precision. The panel blinked green this time, and the door slid open with a soft hiss.

He slipped through the door, the alarm now a distant echo. Inside the new section, the hum of machinery was louder and more pronounced. He knew he was getting closer to the collider. Before stepping in, he sent a final text:

>Reaper

Moving forward.

* * *

Dr. Evelyn Shaw stood in the cramped office of Dr. Anya Petrova, her face a mask of steely determination. The room was cluttered with stacks of research papers, diagrams, and scientific models. A dim desk lamp cast a soft glow, barely illuminating the tension that hung thick in the air.

"Anya, you have to listen to me," she implored, her voice low but intense. "Weiss isn't driven by scientific curiosity or the betterment of humanity. He's reckless, and his vision for the LHC... it's a catastrophe waiting to happen."

Dr. Petrova, seated behind her desk, looked up at her with a mixture of confusion and frustration. Her delicate features were pinched with worry, her usually pristine lab coat rumpled. She ran a hand through her short, blond hair, shaking her head.

"Evelyn, I understand your concerns, but this isn't the way to handle it," Dr. Petrova replied, her voice trembling slightly. "Weiss may be ambitious, but he's brilliant. The work we're doing here... it's groundbreaking. It's what you wanted. Project Exodia was *your* idea. How can you back out now and point fingers?"

Jeremiah, the veteran engineer and technician, stood leaning against the wall, his arms crossed over his broad chest. His face was stern, his jaw set tight as he listened to the exchange. His presence added an unspoken pressure to the room.

"It's not about backing out or being afraid of progress," she insisted, her tone urgent. "It's about the consequences we're already seeing. The anomalies, the breaches—they're not just minor side effects. They're signs that we're meddling with forces we don't fully understand, forces that could destroy us all."

Dr. Petrova's eyes widened, a flash of fear crossing her face before she masked it with a forced calm. "Evelyn, you're overreacting. Every scientific breakthrough comes with risks. We can't let fear hold us back."

Dr. Shaw stepped closer, leaning over Dr. Petrova's desk. "This isn't just about risks. It's about recklessness. Weiss is willing to sacrifice anything and anyone for his vision. I've seen the data. The breaches are getting worse and more unpredictable. If we don't shut this down now, we could be opening a door to something we can't close."

Dr. Petrova looked between Dr. Shaw and Jeremiah, the internal conflict evident on her face. "I... I want to believe you, but this project... it's everything I've, uh, *we've* worked for."

Dr. Shaw's expression softened slightly, but her resolve remained firm. "I know, Anya. I know how much this means to you. But sometimes, the greatest act of courage is knowing when to stop. We need to prioritize humanity's safety over scientific ambition."

Dr. Petrova looked down at her hands, her fingers trembling. She took a deep breath, lifting her gaze to meet her colleagues. "I'd rather you leave now, Dr. Shaw. We're on the brink of something bigger than all of us combined, and I refuse to let you hold us back."

Her eyes widened at Dr. Petrova's words, a distinct sadness flashing across her face. "Anya, I-"

"You've always told me what to do and what not to; I'm not your subordinate anymore, and I am not authorizing to shut the collider off. Mr. Smith?" she turned her eyes to Jeremiah, who was still standing against the wall. "Please continue as scheduled; Dr. Weiss will return from his business trip in two days, and he expects results."

The man nodded, pushing himself off the wall as he began to walk out with an exasperated Dr. Shaw behind him. She yelled at him in frustration, asking why he wouldn't understand what she was saying. And he, ever the face of stoicism, sighed, turning around to give her a cold stare.

"Because, *Dr. Shaw*, I am not going to stick my neck out for the likes of anyone, not again; not anymore," he replied, eyes bearing a hint of the turmoil he carried within.

"Jeremy, please. I promise. It's not li-"

"Oh, for God's sake; listen to yourself, Eve!" He snapped, rubbing his hand over his face. "It's always the same with you. You just want your work done, and guess what; so does Weiss. The only difference is we all know he's a turd since he doesn't hide it, and you tend to leave people stranded and shut them out once shit hits the fan. So, just, *please*, cut the crap, okay?"

Dr. Evelyn Shaw stood in the bright corridor, watching Jeremiah's broad back as he walked away. She took a deep breath, knowing that she had to keep trying. Her heart ached at his words - mostly because he was being truthful. The collider had been her passion…her obsession, and she had placed everything below it. Her fears, her feelings, and even her relationships. She had distanced herself from everyone and everything, believing that she didn't need anyone once she successfully had *Exodia*. It was what her beloved, late mother, Dr. Abishola Shaw, would've wanted. Perhaps, she thought, wiping the tears trickling down her cheeks, she ought to call her father.

Just to see how he was doing, given the possible doomed fate of humanity and all that. Professor Robert Shaw, a retired historian, would be intrigued by it all if she were to tell him.

With that thought still swirling in her mind, she made her way to the section of the facility where the extended machinery and pods were stored. The metallic hum of the facility grew louder as she approached the bio-mechanical section, the air tinged with the scent of disinfectant and machinery. As she stepped inside the room, her eyes adjusted to the dim light, focusing on the intricate network of machinery and transparent pods that housed the nano-robotic shards. The sight was both awe-inspiring and terrifying—a show of human ingenuity.

She noticed a fellow scientist already in the room, standing by one of the transparent pods, observing the nano-robotic shards inside. He was middle-aged with the kind of put-together appearance that was almost unusual for most doctors there, given their long, unreasonable working hours. The lab coat was slightly too snug for his sturdy, muscular frame. Evelyn didn't recognize him, which was strange given her familiarity with most of the staff in this section. At the very least, she would've seen him once or twice in the past.

The man blinked at her a couple of times, his expression awkward as he greeted her with a hesitant nod. "Uh, hello," he said, his voice wavering slightly. "I didn't expect anyone else to be here."

Her instincts tingled with unease. There was something off about him, something that didn't quite fit. She was about to ask his name when her phone buzzed in her pocket. She pulled it out and saw a text from Nadia:

Uncle's contact sent in a tip. One of our own has breached security codes and is inside the bio-mechanical section.

Evelyn's heart rate quickened as she looked back at the stranger. Could this be the person Marcus was talking about? Another potential ally or a threat in disguise?

She took a step closer, "I don't believe we've met. I'm Dr. Evelyn Shaw. And you are...?"

The man swallowed nervously, his eyes darting around the room before meeting hers. "I'm Dr. David Hargrove. I, uh, recently transferred here from the East Coast facility."

Evelyn's gaze remained unwavering. "Is that so? And what exactly are you doing here, Dr. Hargrove?"

He shifted uncomfortably, his hands fidgeting with the hem of his lab coat. "I'm, uh, conducting a preliminary analysis of the nano-robotic shards. Dr. Weiss assigned me to this task."

Evelyn's suspicion deepened. She knew that Weiss was known for bringing in outside help, but he usually informed her of any new additions to the team. "I see. Well, Dr. Hargrove, you'll understand if I verify your credentials with Dr. Weiss. Security is a top priority here."

Before she could reach for her phone to make the call, the man held up his hands in a placating gesture. "Wait, there's no need for that. I can explain everything."

She arched an eyebrow, waiting for him to continue. "I'm not really Dr. Hargrove," he admitted, his voice dropping to a whisper. "I'm John Harrows. I've been working with Phoenix to uncover the truth about this facility. I used the codes Phoenix sent me to get in here."

Evelyn's eyes widened slightly. "John Harrows? I- wait, I remember you. You were the highest-ranking officer when we were moving the machinery from South Carolina to here. There was a whole issue about you making a fuss about how the generators were to be transported."

John nodded, his expression earnest. "Yes, and now I'm here to help. This...whatever all this is, is related to the Cabal. I'm sure of it."

"I'm sorry; the *what?*"

John looked down at his phone when Phoenix messaged him once more.

>Phoenix

Evelyn Shaw. Ally. BigRedStud. Ally. Nadia Ayoub. Ally.

He sighed, grateful that he needn't worry about threatening her if she refused to cooperate. He then explained the Cabal briefly to her, mentioning the global anomalies and the Cabal's links to almost every large, profitable firm or chain across the world, regardless of industry. Even well-known politicians, other professionals, and celebrities were a part of this cult.

Evelyn took a moment to process this revelation.

John's shoulders relaxed slightly, relief evident on his face. "So, we need to be careful. If we get caught, it's military prison for us, and trust me, it's not pretty."

She nodded, "And what of this Phoenix? Mr. Flynn mentioned this person, too. Do you have any way of getting them to meet us?"

"None at all. But I'm sure you can get them to help if you give information about Cabal in return. This isn't just your fight, you know."

* * *

Zara sat on the edge of a creaky bed, the dim yellow light from the bedside lamp casting long shadows around the room. Despite it being midday, the sun had barely come out, and with the blinds pulled in front, there was hardly any natural light. The worn-out motel room smelled faintly of cleaning supplies and old fabric. She balanced her laptop on her knees, fingers flying across the keys as lines of code scrolled up the screen.

Her setup was simple but effective: a laptop connected to a portable Wi-Fi hotspot, a small notepad filled with scribbled notes and coordinates, and a phone on silent mode beside her. The past few days had been a whirlwind of clandestine messages and covert operations, all culminating in this moment.

She had successfully guided Reaper—John Harrows—into the research facility using the codes she'd decrypted and sent him. Now, she anxiously awaited an update from him. The plan hinged on his ability to navigate the facility undetected and link her to the mainframe via his phone. She trusted his military precision but knew the risks were high.

Zara took a deep breath and glanced at her phone; still no word from John. She couldn't help but think of the other operative, BigRedStud, whose true identity was shrouded in layers of binary security. Unlike John, whose identity she had uncovered, BigRedStud remained an enigma. His fake IP had been cleverly crafted, but she knew he was essential to their mission.

As she waited, Zara's mind wandered to the recent developments. The anomalies, the LHC, the potential for disaster—everything pointed to a conspiracy of unprecedented scale. Her brother Faisal's death still haunted her, driving her to uncover the truth at any cost.

She hoped that by exposing the secrets of the LHC and the Cabal, she could bring justice and prevent further tragedy.

A soft chime from her laptop snapped her back to the present. A message from John:

>Reaper

Inside. Reached control room. Ready to link mainframe.

Her heart skipped a beat. This was it. She quickly typed back:

>Phoenix

Link me to the mainframe. I'll take it from there. Stay alert.

Moments later, a new window popped up on her screen, indicating that John had successfully connected his phone to the facility's mainframe. Zara's fingers danced over the keys, bypassing firewalls and security protocols with practiced ease. She could see the intricate network of the facility's systems, data streams, and access points.

She initiated a deeper probe, her screen filling with a cascade of code and system diagrams. She was in. The real work began now—extracting data, finding incriminating evidence, and ensuring they had what they needed to expose the truth. All the while making sure that nothing could be traced back to her. This meant that as soon as this was done, she'd have to throw away the burner phone she had been using to contact him and move locations.

>Phoenix

Updates will be provided.

* * *

Dr. Shaw watched in utter awe at the humungous panels and screens in the control room where she had led Harrows to, as per his request and Marcus' guarantee to, trust anyone using Phoenix's reference.

He had used the wireless port to connect a new, pristine-looking device to the panel, having first connected to his other phone. After that, it took only a few moments until the screen was overrun by never-ending columns and rows of codes.

By then, Marcus had been escorted by Nadia to the room as well. She, taking caution, had decided to stay out of the mechanical doorway as a way to warn them beforehand of anyone walking in on them.

Marcus stepped further into the room, his eyes adjusting to the dim lighting. He spotted Dr. Evelyn Shaw, who was standing next to a man he instantly recognized from the files he had combed through. It was Colonel John Harrows, one of the military personnel assigned to the safety of transporting the LHC to the New Dawn Facility. Both Shade and Phoenix had really come through; he wasn't expecting this level of cooperation from a pair of probable virtual terrorists.

John looked up, his eyes narrowing as he assessed the newcomer. Marcus could see the caution and readiness in his stance, the telltale signs of a trained soldier. Evelyn, noticing the tension, waved a hand.

"Mr. Flynn," she said with the first hints of what could almost be considered a smile, "this is Colonel John Harrows. Colonel, this is Marcus Flynn, an investigative journalist who's been trying to uncover the truth about the anomalies and the LHC."

Harrows extended a hand, his grip firm. "A journalist, huh? You one of those truth seekers?"

Marcus nodded, shaking his hand. "I've been following the breadcrumbs. And your name came up in my research, Colonel. Your background in the military and your assignment here at the facility."

Harrows raised an eyebrow. "You've done your homework. But what exactly brings you here?"

"The same birdie that's led you here, Phoenix."

"Let me guess; you're BigRedStud? I mean, I can see why I had trouble pinpointing you," Harrows smirked, making a jab at Marcus' rather stocky frame next to the titan that was Harrows.

Before Marcus could respond, Dr. Shaw interjected. "John, we need your help. The LHC isn't just a scientific experiment—it's a portal, and it's causing dangerous breaches. There was something that reached out the first time we had powered it up. And now, with everything that's happening around the world because of it, we must act fast." She paused, looking at him with pleading eyes. "We *need* to shut it down, but Weiss won't allow it. Your expertise and our contact, Phoenix's skills, are crucial."

As if on cue, Marcus' phone buzzed with a message from Phoenix.

>Phoenix

This will take a while. Can't continue in one place for too long. Will contact once location is shifted.

Marcus sighed, conveying the message to the other two, making a mental note to connect Shade to Phoenix. Perhaps the two working together might be able to get this done quicker.

"You know, this is less of an exposure mission and more of a complete takedown," Marcus pointed, finally digging into his jeans pocket and retrieving a cigarette. Lighting it up despite Dr. Shaw's scrunched nose, he inhaled deeply.

"Clearly. Phoenix will figure out how the Cabal is involved in this, and then I'll have to get to them the old-fashioned style."

"Calm down, Rambo. You casn't just waltz in and slash them to bits," Marcus muttered, making Harrows glare at him.

"If it's all linked," Dr. Shaw spoke again, trying to keep the peace. "Then we'll have to come up with a very substantial strategy to ensure we get rid of this organization so this issue can be stopped for good. Because let's be honest," she paused to run a hand in her frizzy but tightly pulled-back hair. "Even if we get rid of the LHC, with the help of those once involved, they could rebuild it, maybe even an improved version in the future."

"Hence, we cut the head off," Harrows added, agreeing with her.

"So, while Phoenix is busy getting into the mainframe, I'll get another contact to see how much he can gather about the Cabal and if he can cough up any names we might find here. Captain Old-Coot here," he grinned, gesturing to Harrows with his thumb, "can plan a good strategy to get inside a possibly military-guarded base since there is no way these gits are out in the open like that."

Harrows' nostrils flared as she glared at Marcus. "And what about you?"

"I told you; *geez*, you're not that old to forget something I *just* said. I'm getting in touch with a contact. And Eve?"

"Yes?" she asked, raising an eyebrow.

"We'll need a place. The kind where no one would expect us to be camping in. A headquarters of sorts to keep everything in one place." Marcus said, blowing out a plume of smoke.

She thought for a second and nodded. "I'll be sure to arrange something as soon as possible. But right now, I'm guessing we will need to leave. It's almost evening, and the operations team will be clocking in soon."

With that settled, the trio made their way outside, where Nadia was sitting on the floor, legs stretched in front of her. Marcus would brief her on everything…and have Shade provide a little extra security to her virtual profile so that no one could target her in case this blew up. Something he was eighty…no, eighty-five percent sure would backfire.

Say the aliens or whatever that's beyond those portals don't get them; that wouldn't stop the government from ruining their lives, and he'd be damned if he let that happen to one of his own.

When Dr. Shaw was about to lead them outside, Harrows stopped her.

"I need to see the collider first," he insisted.

She hesitated. "It's dangerous, and we don't have much time."

Harrows shook his head. "I need to see it for myself to understand what we're dealing with."

With a reluctant nod, she agreed. "Alright, but be quick. Mr. Flynn, continue with Nadia. I'll take Harrows to the collider."

Marcus gave her a curt nod, turning back to Nadia, who had now stood up. Dr. Shaw and Harrows made their way through the winding corridors to the collider chamber.

The door to the collider room slid open with a soft hiss, revealing the massive machinery within. The LHC's structure loomed like a sleeping giant, its intricate network of wires and circuits glowing faintly. The hum of power was a constant background noise, a reminder of the immense energy contained within.

He stepped forward, his eyes scanning the machinery. "This is it," he muttered, a mix of awe and dread in his voice.

She nodded. "Yes. Again, we have to be careful."

As she spoke, a sudden flash of electricity sparked by the machines. Dr. Shaw instinctively stepped back, her heart racing. The wires began to whir, emitting an eerie, high-pitched noise.

"What's happening?" He asked, his eyes narrowing.

"I don't know," she admitted, her voice tinged with fear. "I'm not a technician."

Before they could react, the air in front of them seemed to shimmer. A small slit appeared in the very fabric of space, growing wider by the second. Their horror grew as a grotesque, sinewy arm reached out from within the void.

She gasped. "We need to shut this down!"

Harrows stepped forward, trying to shield her. "Stand back."

The arm continued to reach through the slit, its fingers grasping at the air. Her heart pounded as she watched, feeling utterly helpless.

As Harrows tried to work the controls, the breach widened, and the arm moved further out. Suddenly, the lights flickered, and the room was plunged into darkness. The red emergency lights flashed, casting eerie shadows across the chamber.

That's when they saw it.

Perched on top of the collider was a horrific creature. Long and twisted, its body was curled unnaturally, bathed in the crimson glow of the emergency lights. She could make out the outlines of an elongated, dog-like snout, yet the figure's body was anthropomorphic, even if grotesquely distorted. It sat with an unnerving stillness; its form twisted in as way that defied natural anatomy.

Harrows stared in horror. There was no reflection where its eyes should have been, but the emergency lights gleamed off its jagged teeth as it snarled like a wild animal. The sound was a low, guttural growl that reverberated through the chamber.

Dr. Shaw felt a wave of terror wash over her. "We need to get out of here," she whispered, her voice barely audible.

Harrows nodded, his eyes never leaving the creature. "Agreed. Slowly."

They began to back away, moving as quietly as possible. The creature's head tilted, following their movements with an unnerving precision. Just as they inched towards the door, it let out a piercing scream, the sound echoing through the facility.

Evelyn and Harrows exchanged a glance filled with fear and determination. They had to warn the others and find a way to stop whatever horror had been unleashed.

But first, they had to make sure that they made it out of the room alive.

The creature slowly moved toward them, its grotesque form creeping forward on all fours like an animal. Its long, sinewy limbs made a sickening sound against the cold floor. The low hisses it emitted were unsettling, each one seeming to pierce the silence and reverberate through the room. Harrows quickly assessed the situation, realizing that the creature might be blind. He stood perfectly still, his eyes locked on its movements. With a slow, deliberate motion, he used his large hand to clasp Dr. Shaw's mouth shut, ensuring she wouldn't even breathe too loudly.

Her eyes were wide with terror, but she was utterly helpless in his grasp and knew that struggling might irk the entity. She could feel his hand trembling slightly, though his grip remained firm. The creature loomed closer, its head twitching as it seemed to listen for them, trying to tune out the sounds of the automated emergency announcements echoing through the speakers. Its elongated snout sniffed the air, its jagged teeth bared in a silent snarl. Harrows knew they had to act fast. His eyes darted to a set of tools placed a few steps away from them—something he could use as a weapon. But retrieving them would mean making a move and potentially alerting the creature to their presence.

The creature paused, its head turning slightly as if it had picked up on something. Harrows held his breath, his mind racing. He needed to be quick and precise. Slowly, he let go of Evelyn's mouth and motioned for her to keep still.

She was too stunned to move…as if her voice box simply refused to work. With that, Harrows waited for the creature to turn its head away, even for a moment.

When it did, he moved. He stepped lightly, timing his steps in a way that he moved each time the automated voice boomed, ensuring that it somewhat masked the sound of his feet. He reached for the tools and quickly grabbed a heavy wrench, his eyes never leaving the creature. Just as he turned back, the creature's head snapped in his direction.

The creature let out a low, menacing growl. He held the wrench tightly, his muscles tense and ready. It began to advance. Harrows knew he had to distract it. He looked at his hand, where a bracelet adorned the wrist. With a swift motion, he threw it across the room, causing it to clatter loudly, drawing the beast's attention. It turned its head toward the noise, giving him the split second he needed. He lunged forward, swinging the wrench with all his might. The wrench connected with the creature's side, producing a sickening crunch. The creature let out a screech of pain, thrashing wildly.

"Run!" He shouted, grabbing her arm and pulling her towards the door.

They sprinted out of the chamber, the creature's agonized screams echoing behind them. Once they were outside, as if snapping back into reality, Dr. Shaw pressed the lockdown from the panel beside the door. The *thing* roared again, this time, its voice sounding a lot like a weeping woman. She felt her stomach churn as she initiated a security procedure, one she had hoped that they never had to use. As she dialed in another code, the doors clasped shut, and tear gas was released into the chamber. Once that was done, they stood there in silence. Unable to tear their eyes away from the giant metal wall.

"What in the ever-loving fuck was that?!" he demanded, wanting to yell, but even his usually booming voice failed him.

"I… I don't know…something not from here," she mumbled, eyes still wide as she held her head. "This is a lot worse than we thought; we don't have any time at this point."

"You're telling me," he muttered, still thinking about what he had just witnessed.

They'd have to tell the others. Warn them quickly. Dr. Shaw's hand trembled as she shakily dialed a number and pressed the phone to her ear. Her breathing hitched as soon as the call connected, tears welling up in her eyes from the shock having worn off.

"Jeremy, please, I need you."

* * *

Despite his usual avoidance of Dr. Shaw, the never seeing each other eye-to-eye, and the pangs of a love that never had the chance to flourish-

Despite it all, Jeremiah Smith didn't waste a single minute in striding down the hallways. He had even brought Thomas along with him. Upon reaching the door, he hesitated, looking at Dr. Shaw's teary eyes. Then, inhaling sharply, he used his special numeric key to override the emergency generator, restoring the room back to the main electricity phase. The fluorescent lights flickered on, casting harsh, sterile light over the scene inside. He unlocked the door, stepping back as it whirred open.

The sight that met them was both horrifying and surreal. The creature was curled up on the floor, lying in a fetal position. Its grotesque form was still, but the air was thick with tension. There was blood spilled near it, and a bloody wrench lay some feet away.

Thomas's eyes widened with surprise, a mixture of fear and excitement playing across his face. "Whoa... what is that?" he whispered, an excited grin forming.

Jeremiah, however, was more cautious. He approached slowly, his eyes narrowing as he studied the creature. "I'm not sure if it's dead," he muttered, his hand resting on the door frame for support.

Dr. Shaw stood behind them, her face pale and tear-streaked. "I activated the security measures," she said, her voice shaking. "Tear gas... it was the only thing I could think of to contain it once Harrows and I got out."

Jeremiah nodded, his eyes never leaving the creature. "Smart move. Let's be careful." He stepped closer, his movements careful. The creature remained still, its twisted body lying in a pool of its own blood.

Thomas moved to the side, his curiosity getting the better of him. "Do you think it's from the other side? Is it an alien? Maybe a demon?" he asked, glancing at Jeremiah.

"Shut up," Jeremiah replied. He reached out with his foot, gently nudging the creature. There was no response. "We can't assume it's dead. Thomas, get the containment unit ready. We need to secure it before it wakes up."

Thomas nodded, running off to fetch the containment unit. Dr. Shaw stepped closer, her eyes locked on the creature. "Jeremiah, I... I don't know how it got through. One moment, the collider wasn't even on, the next... this."

Jeremiah put a reassuring hand on her shoulder. "We'll figure it out, Eve. First, we need to make sure this thing doesn't pose any more danger."

Thomas returned with the containment unit…which was a large transparent pod of sorts set atop a fully automated transporting robot.

The robotic arms reached out to pick the creature up and place it inside, sealing it shut and loading it onto the carrier once more.

"I'll go get Nadia to attach the vital tubes to it," Thomas said, starting to follow the robot out while paging her.

Jeremiah turned to Dr. Shaw, his expression serious. "We need to report this immediately. Dr. Weiss needs to know what's happened."

She shook her head. "No, Jeremy. Don't you get it; this is exactly what he wants! We can't let him know of this. God knows what he'll do!"

"Well, you can't just hide it," Jeremiah said, shaking his head and glancing at Harrows, who was picking up the wrench.

"Just a bit more time so that we can get the information through our livewires and get into the real people who want to continue using this monstrosity," she replied, feeling a headache starting to come.

"Okay, just, let's get you some rest. We can talk about this later. Tommy and I; we'll keep our lips zipped, okay?" Jeremiah said, hoping to calm her down as he gently steered her out of the room, paging for a cleanup crew and reporting it as a common accident.

Harrows followed close behind, pocketing the wrench in his too-snug of a lab coat.

In all his years, never had he ever seen anything like that, nor was he sure if anything could've prepared him for it. He needed some downtime. A lift to go see Max.

Anything besides being here. While he walked behind the two, he sent an important update.

>Reaper

You're not gonna believe what I saw.

Chapter 4: Crossing the Thresholds

Nadia stood by the control panel in Containment Unit 07, her fingers hovering over the touchpad as she made precise adjustments. Her face mirrored her concentration, eyes scanning the myriad of data displayed on the screen. The translucent pod holding the entity was placed a mere foot away, filled with hydration and anti-fungal fluids to maintain the cleanliness of the tanks.

Thomas stood behind her, his gaze shifting between her and the pod. His expression was one of awe, though the evidence of slight fear had managed to seep through.

"Can you believe it, Nadia?" he said, his voice barely above a whisper. "We're standing here with something from another dimension. It's like Star Wars."

She nodded, her focus never leaving the control panel. "Except George Lucas didn't direct this; he's real, and he's dangerous."

He watched as she accessed the pod's integrated monitoring system. The screen displayed a series of complex graphs and biometric data, each representing a different aspect of the creature's physiology.

Nadia glanced at the vital signs, noting the creature's heart rate, respiration, and brain activity. "He's alive, alright," she murmured, a slight edge to her voice. "Jeremiah was right."

Thomas leaned in closer, almost hovering over her with eyes wide with interest. "Look at those readings. The heart rate is similar to a human, but the respiration pattern is completely different."

She adjusted a few more settings, her mind racing with possibilities. "It's almost like he's adapted to our environment. The atmosphere, the pressure, and even the temperature. It's remarkable."

Tapping a few more keys, she initiated a detailed scan. The pod emitted a soft whir as the sensors conducted their analysis, projecting a three-dimensional hologram of the creature above the control panel. The hologram rotated slowly, revealing the entity's sinewy form in stark detail.

He stared at the hologram. "It's like nothing I've ever seen. The anatomy... it's both familiar and alien."

Nadia nodded, her eyes narrowing as she studied the creature's elongated limbs and twisted features. "There's a certain symmetry to it, but it's also... unsettling. The way he's supposed to move, he's designed for stealth and speed. No eyes, so he's either nocturnal or just lives in a dark habitat; maybe damp too, given the lack of fiber on his skin."

Thomas frowned, his fingers tapping nervously on the edge of the control panel. "Do you think it poses a threat?"

"No, Thomas, I don't think a seven-foot-tall demonic-looking thing with a snout and no eyes could ever possibly be a threat," she answered sarcastically, rolling her eyes at him. "I'm sure he just wants to sit and play fetch or something."

Thomas' fair face flushed pink with embarrassment. "You don't have to be mean about it; I was just asking," he huffed, crossing his arms.

She adjusted the panel again, switching the display to focus on the creature's neural activity. The patterns were erratic, unlike anything she had seen before. "His brain activity is off the charts. He's processing information at an incredible rate. I think he can hear us even from the pod," she muttered, adding that theory to the observation notes accessible on the panel's data entry system.

"Isn't this glass bulletproof or something?" Thomas inquired, unable to resist any longer as he tapped on the glass with his index finger.

Almost immediately, the heartbeat and brain activity readings went up. Nadia whipped her head around to glare at him. "Thomas, for goodness' sake, you're making him anxious. He 'sees' via his auditory and olfactory senses."

Thomas stopped, looking at her with a raised eyebrow. "Him? What, you're already on a familiar basis with it?" Before she could say anything, he turned his gaze to the data, adding, "Do you think it understands what's happening?"

Nadia hesitated, her eyes flicking from the screen to the pod. "It's hard to say. But if he's as intelligent as these readings suggest, we need to proceed with caution."

He turned his attention back to the pod, his fascination growing. "What's our next move?"

She took a step back from the control panel, her mind weighing the options. "First, we secure this data. It's compulsory that we have a comprehensive record of his vitals and behavior. Then, we need to consider the ethical implications of what we've discovered."

Thomas nodded, his enthusiasm momentarily tempered by the gravity of the situation. "And Dr. Shaw?"

Nadia sighed, glancing at the lab's entrance. "She'll want to be informed of everything. This is her project, after all, and she'll know the best course of action. Until then, I just have to make sure he's okay."

Thomas' stare flickered from the panel to her and then to the pod, where the creature's sensory orifices had been protected via metallic, padded coverings to ensure the fluids did not seep through. The tubes attached to them could then be used to communicate with it. He shook his head when Nadia took the liberty of naming it in the records. His mind drifted to the possibilities of what else could be out there: intelligent and wise beings like Vulcans? Martians? Maybe even a whole computerized planet like New Genesis? Or, he sighed, closing his eyes-

Perhaps what he was once taught to be Hell?

Is that where something like that could've crawled out from? He didn't know, but he hoped that, on the off chance he did find out, it wasn't at the expense of his sanity.

* * *

The oppressive heat of the midday sun beat down on the corrugated metal roofs of Barangay Macopa, a low-income neighborhood nestled along the coastline of Manila. The air was humid, carrying the pungent scents of saltwater and diesel fumes from the nearby fishing boats. In the heart of this bustling community lay a dilapidated building that once housed a thriving arcade, now long abandoned and repurposed for furtive (and often illegal) activities. Its chipped paint and shattered windows bore witness to years of neglect, but for Viktor "Shade" Vasiliev, it was the perfect hideout.

Inside the arcade, the room was dimly lit by the glow of computer screens and a lone fluorescent light flickering above. Dust clung to every surface, and the air was stagnant, save for the hum of electronics and the occasional creak of the aging structure. Rows of obsolete arcade machines lined the walls, their once-vibrant decals now faded and peeling. The sounds of waves crashing against the shore were faintly audible, a constant reminder of the world outside.

In the corner of the room, Shade sat hunched over a sleek laptop, his fingers flying across the keyboard. The screen before him displayed the complex schematics of the Large Hadron Collider at the New Dawn facility. Lines of code scrolled rapidly as he meticulously mapped out the inner workings of the LHC, each keystroke bringing him closer to uncovering its secrets.

Shade was…strange, for lack of a better term. He had the kind of demeanor that suggested he could vanish into thin air at a moment's notice. His bony, lean frame was clad in a plain black t-shirt and worn cargo pants, hair shaved close to his scalp, accentuating the sharp angles of his face. But it was his eyes that drew the most attention — cold, piercing, and always assessing.

A few yards away from Shade, his acquaintance lounged in an old office chair, balancing precariously on its back two legs. One of his own legs rested on the chair's arm, the other dangled lazily, occasionally tapping against the cracked tiles below. An industrial fan mounted on the wall to his left whirred at a thunderous speed. Despite the probable discomfort from the noise, both men appeared unfazed, focused entirely on the task at hand.

His screen flickered with a series of profiles, each one accompanied by a dossier and a grainy photograph, which soon transitioned into a high-definition image. It was a comprehensive list of all personnel affiliated with the New Dawn facility, from esteemed scientists to lowly janitors. The acquaintance, a wiry man with a quick wit and an even quicker temper, squinted at the information, making mental notes as he went along. This was Cho, a streetwise, tech-savvy individual who had carved out a niche for himself in the world of digital espionage. And one whose real name remained so elusive that Shade, at times, wondered if he even had one.

Cho tapped on the keyboard, skimming through background checks and security clearances. Shade had instructed him to leave no stone unturned, emphasizing the importance of identifying potential threats and allies alike. But one profile stood out above the rest—Nadia Ayoub, Marcus Flynn's niece. Shade had made it clear that her file was to be given extra scrutiny, a request that promised a handsome reward.

He yawned, resting back into his odd position on the chair as the pictures and profile loaded. The information was thorough yet mundane; nothing immediately jumped out as suspicious or noteworthy. But Shade trusted Marcus, and Marcus trusted her, which meant he had to dig deeper, all the while creating a few layers of extra virtual security for her. And as per logic, even a self-deletion to erase her off the databases should shit hit the fan for them.

"How's the girl looking?" Shade asked without looking up, his voice low and gravelly, as though it hadn't been used in a while. The sound of his words was punctuated by the clack of keys.

"Way too good to be related to Flynn," Cho replied, tilting his head before his neck snapped from the unnatural position he was seated in. "She's clean, though. But her security clearance is higher than I expected for someone at her level. Might be worth looking into."

Shade nodded, a small smirk playing at the corners of his lips. "Means she's in deep; no wonder he wants her off the radar."

Cho returned his attention to the screen, checking for any anomalies or inconsistencies that could hint at hidden agendas. Shade, meanwhile, focused on the LHC's intricate design, his eyes narrowed at what he was seeing. Marcus' request was not one he took lightly. A sense of triumph washed over him as he surveyed the digital landscape. This was it—the Holy Grail of the collider's secrets laid bare in a series of diagrams, codes, and confidential documents. The culmination of endless hours of coding had finally revealed the very core of the LHC.

The screen displayed a multi-layered blueprint that mapped out the entirety of the collider. It was an awe-inspiring sight, a sprawling network of tunnels and chambers that stretched miles beneath the North Dakota plains. The inner levels of the collider were revealed in meticulous detail, showcasing a structure that was as much a fortress as it was a scientific instrument. Each section was annotated with notes on its purpose and function, all of which painted a picture of an extraordinary scientific endeavor.

At the heart of the LHC was the main accelerator ring, a circular tunnel nearly 27 kilometers in circumference that housed superconducting magnets and particle beams. These beams, comprising protons and heavy ions, were propelled to near-light speeds, colliding at precise points to create conditions akin to those at the universe's birth. The sheer power and energy encapsulated within this ring were staggering.

The blueprint also showcased the array of sensors and detectors positioned around the ring, each designed to capture the smallest particle interactions. Shade studied the advanced technologies integrated into the system, including the cryogenic cooling units essential for maintaining the superconducting state of the magnets.

Adjacent to the main ring were the collision chambers—massive caverns carved out to host the most powerful particle collisions ever conceived. The chambers were equipped with detectors capable of recording minute details of each collision event. These detectors were not merely passive instruments but rather sophisticated networks designed to parse through enormous volumes of data in real-time, identifying patterns and anomalies with precision.

Shade noted the presence of a chamber labeled "The Nexus." This chamber was distinct, both in size and purpose, designed for Project Exodia—a classified initiative within the LHC aimed at exploring multi-dimensional phenomena. This was where the theoretical intersected with the physical, where the fabric of reality itself was tested. The files hinted at experiments beyond standard particle physics ventures into realms of dark matter and alternate dimensions.

"Pizdec…" he mumbled to himself, straightening his back against the chair. "Bastard wasn't kidding; shit's all messed up."

Below the collision chambers lay a series of subterranean research facilities accessible through a network of passageways and elevator shafts. These levels were home to labs that conducted various ancillary experiments, each with a unique focus on pushing the boundaries of known science. The blueprints showed restricted areas within these labs, marked with ominous warnings and encrypted access codes that suggested the presence of dangerous or highly confidential research.

One section caught Shade's attention—a series of interconnected labs dedicated to the study of bio-mechanical integration and nano-robotics. These labs were tasked with developing technology to harness the energies released in particle collisions, potentially creating new materials or even forms of life. It was a venture that walked the fine line between innovation and ethical transgression, indicative of Dr. Anton Weiss' more ambitious (and possibly nefarious) vision for the LHC.

Deeper still was the Theoretical Physics Wing, a place where the abstract theories that governed the collider's operation were born and refined. This wing housed teams of scientists working tirelessly to decode the mysteries of the universe, armed with powerful computers that ran simulations of cosmic events. The files Shade accessed contained outlines of several groundbreaking theories, including the much-debated concept of parallel dimensions.

One particularly dense document outlined Project Exodia's theoretical framework, positing the existence of multiple realities that could potentially intersect with our own. The document suggested that the collider might, under specific conditions, open a rift- a controlled tear in the fabric of space-time, leading to phenomena whose results were undetermined.

The blueprints also laid bare the facility's robust security measures. A range of biometric scanners, automated defenses, and emergency protocols were in place to protect against both internal and external threats. Shade noted the presence of several fail-safes designed to neutralize the collider's operations in case of a breach, though the efficacy of such measures was questionable given the magnitude of the forces at play. Of particular interest were the containment protocols for 'anomalous entities,' mentioned in a series of encrypted files. This newly added segment outlined procedures for handling breaches that involved biological or multi-dimensional anomalies, hinting at recent incidents that had necessitated such measures. The revelation was chilling, suggesting that the facility had already encountered and perhaps even captured entities from beyond our understanding.

As he absorbed this wealth of information, he couldn't help but be slightly unnerved by it all. It seemed too unreal. The idea that this thing was not only up and running but had potentially managed to keep some souvenirs? It was genuinely frightening even to someone like him. The New Dawn facility and its LHC project were far more than a scientific pursuit; they were a precipice, teetering on the edge of profound discovery and catastrophic failure. Shade understood that his role in this unfolding drama was pivotal.

Just as he was about to link to Marcus, Cho's screen beeped, causing Shade to turn around and narrow his eyes at it.

"Someone got into the place's mainframe, trying to flush us from the system," he said as Shade stood up from his spot and walked towards the other screen. His legs wobbled from hours of being bent in the same position.

"We've got what we needed," Cho muttered, aborting the system and coding the program to get a 'look' at the third party that had crashed their little mission. "But," he paused, sitting upright as he continued to ferociously tap on the keys. "I want to see you," he mumbled to no one in particular.

* * *

In another remote motel on the outskirts of Fargo, Zara Akhtar sat at a small wooden desk that barely held her state-of-the-art laptop and an array of cables and gadgets sprawled across its surface. The only other light source aside from her screen was a single table lamp set on a worn, wooden nightstand. Outside, the wind howled through the empty corridors of the motel, creating a spooky backdrop to the intense digital battle that was unfolding inside.

Zara pressed the keys with a dexterity honed from years of experience. Her screen was an exhibition of code and data streams, each line telling a story only a virtual creature of the night could understand. She was deep into the mainframe of the New Dawn Facility, the covert research lab known for its controversial Large Hadron Collider project. The information she had access to was a treasure trove of secrets and classified files, offering a glimpse into the heart of a scientific enigma. But that was not what she was there for. She needed to cross check it with the info she had on the Cabal in order to weed out which members of the facility doubled as Cabal agents.

But as she worked, she encountered something unexpected—a presence in the system that was neither part of the facility's defenses nor her own doing. Zara's eyes narrowed as she stared at the screen, recognizing the signs of a third-party intrusion. Whoever it was, they were skilled, and their presence was almost ethereal, like a ghost in the machine.

Her fingers moved faster, executing commands to isolate and identify the intruder. As she dug deeper, she realized this was no ordinary hacker. The digital signature was masked by layers of encryption and proxies, each one more complex than the last. This wasn't just another government or corporate firewall—this was someone with serious skills, perhaps even on par with her own.

Zara felt a chill run down her spine, a sense of foreboding that something was about to go awry. Suddenly, the hacker on the other side made their move, launching a minor yet precise attack that slipped through her defenses like a knife through butter. Her system beeped, alerting her that data had been accessed, but she couldn't immediately tell what had been compromised.

A string of curses escaped her lips as she launched into overdrive, fingers flying over the keyboard. She activated a series of aggressive countermeasures designed to overwhelm and disorient her digital opponent. Firing off a sequence of brute-force attacks aimed at penetrating their defenses and tracking them back to their origin. The screen flickered as data streams collided in a fierce cyber-duel. Assuming that this was the Cabal, she was determined to flush them out and gain control of the system, hoping to use their own hub against them.

As she pushed forward, she initiated a series of harsh attacks that pounded at the intruder's digital walls. Her goal was simple: force them to reboot their entire system, rendering them vulnerable and buying her time to secure her own data. The air was thick with tension as she watched the lines of code scroll across the screen, each one a barrage in her digital offensive.

Suddenly, the enemy's defenses crumbled under her relentless onslaught. Her terminal flashed as she penetrated deeper into their system, her algorithms carving paths through the tangled web of their security protocols. She could almost taste victory, believing she had cornered one of the Cabal's agents.

As the dust settled in the virtual arena, Zara leaned back in her chair, taking a moment to catch her breath. Her eyes flickered across the screen, scanning for any remnants of the intruder's presence. There was nothing but the reassuring glow of her own system, now secure and fortified against further incursions. Despite her apparent success, Zara couldn't shake the feeling of unease that lingered in the room. The thought that someone had managed to breach her defenses, even momentarily, gnawed at her. What data had been stolen, if any? What information had been exposed to those prying eyes?

The motel room was silent except for the soft hum of her laptop. Zara knew she had to remain vigilant; the stakes were too high to let her guard down. Sighing, she reached out to check one of the temporary phones she used. Some texts from Harrows and BigRedStud were displayed on the screen. The latter informed her of the current proceedings, including an updated list of allies and a request to meddle with the security footage as required, ensuring that their affairs remained a secret. However, it was Harrows' message that made her raise an eyebrow.

* * *

>Phoenix

Try me.

John Harrows groaned, shifting from his position on the mattress when he noticed the ping coming from his phone. Taking it in his hand, he squinted at the message before sighing and sitting up, resting his back against the headboard. His body felt limp, plagued by an acute feverish temperature. He reckoned it was the sudden stress after encountering that entity that had caused it. Sighing, he requested an audio channel, insisting that what he wanted to tell was far too detailed to be typed out.

Phoenix's response was quick, informing him that they were setting up a voice channel for them to access. Once the link came through, Harrows placed the phone on speaker and waited until the microphone on the other end was active.

"Speak!" The artificially altered voice demanded as soon as the connection was established.

Harrows didn't protest, going into details about what he had seen, how it came to be, and what became of it. When he was done, he waited for the other's response. For a few minutes, there was complete silence on Phoenix's side. Then the audio disconnected, and a single-worded text message popped up:

>Phoenix

Interesting.

He shook his head, continuing to chat.

>Reaper

Anything on your end?

>Phoenix

I'm in the mainframe, laying low. The Cabal was in. Saw another unauthorized signature in the system. Threat eliminated for now. Minor data loss. Nothing serious. Security footage at New Dawn compromised as per BigRedStud's request.

>Reaper

Okay. Will keep you posted. The security footage would show you the Thing, too. Get a good idea. We've changed house.

>Phoenix

 Understood.

>Reaper

Stay safe.

And just like that, the chat box became inaccessible, indicating that Phoenix had signed off. Harrows placed the back of his hand against his forehead, feeling the heat radiating from his skin. He hadn't anticipated getting sick, but there he was, at their new headquarters, which was essentially Dr. Shaw's old family home. It was currently empty as her father had moved in with her uncle in Illinois; not that any of them, aside from the doctor and Jeremiah, knew that fact.

Placing the phone on the bedside table, Harrows laid back down, hoping that some rest would help calm his nerves. There was too much to be done for him to be out of commission due to a fever.

Outside, in the overgrown backyard, Marcus Flynn sat on the steps of the backdoor that connected the yard to the kitchen inside. A cigarette smoldering between his fingers as he blew out a puff of smoke. Harrow's dog, Max, was busy lapping up his dinner from the dog dish, which was placed some spaces beside Marcus.

His thoughts were jumbled, and he found it extremely difficult to focus, thinking of everything yet unable to understand anything at the moment. Maisie, his wife, would often joke that she wished he had come with a remote control so she could turn his brain off for a while. A small, sad smile tugged at his lips as he inhaled the cigarette.

Maybe, he thought, he'd try. Really try to win her back after this fiasco was taken care of.

* * *

The small room was cluttered with wires and gadgets, and the air reeked with the smell of takeout containers and coffee. The motel's outdated furnishings were barely noticeable to Zara, who was entirely absorbed in her digital surveillance work. She sat cross-legged on the bed, her laptop perched precariously on a stack of old newspapers. The light from the screen cast a bluish glow on her features, highlighting the intensity of her gaze.

The footage played out silently in front of her, with the occasional flicker of static as she fast-forwarded and rewound different feeds. Her fingers deftly tapped the keyboard as she paused on a particular segment—an angle capturing the translucent pod where the entity was being held. The feed showed the events that had transpired earlier when Nadia Ayoub was in the room with Thomas Anderson. The sight of the entity encased in the pod was unsettling, its hideous form barely contained within the transparent enclosure.

Zara watched closely as Thomas departed, leaving Nadia alone with the pod. Nadia lingered there longer than expected, her expression unreadable as she stood by the containment unit. Zara narrowed her eyes, noticing a slight tremor in her hand as she reached into her coat pocket. The camera angle didn't provide a clear view of what Nadia retrieved, but Zara saw her discreetly introduce something into one of the input tubes connected to the pod.

"The bloody hell are you up to?" Zara muttered under her breath, replaying the scene a few times to ensure she hadn't missed anything. Despite her best efforts, she couldn't discern what Nadia had slipped into the tube or what its intended purpose might be. Zara filed the observation away for later analysis; her curiosity was piqued but not distracted from her primary objective.

Satisfied that she had gathered all relevant information from Nadia's interaction with the pod, Zara fast-forwarded the footage to the present moment. The digital timestamp ticked away in the corner of the screen as she scanned through hours of uneventful footage. The facility seemed to be operating smoothly, with personnel going about their duties as expected. The lab's segment where the creature had been kept was clearly sealed off from the rest of the department, given how, despite the other workers there, none had come to that specific area. Satisfied, she stored the footage in her personally crafted cloud and got rid of it from the facility's database before moving to review other compartments.

But something caught her eye—a feed from the LHC chamber. The camera captured an unusual occurrence: sparks flashing across the outer panel and frame of the massive collider. At first glance, it appeared to be a simple electrical malfunction, perhaps a result of the facility's aged infrastructure. But as she scrutinized the footage, a creeping unease settled in her stomach. The sparks didn't dissipate. Instead, they seemed to intensify, a ghostly luminescence. Zara's fingers flew across the keyboard, zooming in and adjusting the resolution to get a better look at what was happening. Her mind raced with possibilities, each one more alarming than the last.

"Cor blimey," she whispered to herself, her heart pounding as the sparks grew brighter. Her instincts told her that this wasn't just a random glitch; something was activating the collider without any human intervention. The realization hit her like a cold wave— whatever was happening, it was deliberate and potentially catastrophic.

Her first thought was to contact Harrows or BigRedStud to alert them to the anomaly she was witnessing. Zara opened a secure messaging app, her fingers flying over the keys as she composed an encrypted message to the latter. The words on the screen were terse yet serious, conveying the situation in just a few lines.

>Phoenix

The collider is active. Zero human interaction.

Meanwhile, across the globe, Shade's hideout remained cloaked in the early morning shadows. The cramped, abandoned arcade was filled with the soft hum of computer equipment and the glow of various monitors displaying feeds and data streams.

In one corner of the room, Cho lay sprawled out on the floor, snoring softly amidst a tangle of cables and discarded soda cans. His sleep was deep and undisturbed. Shade himself was seated at his main workstation, now with a series of high-definition monitors displayed before him. He was intensely focused, his eyes locked onto a specific set of images on one of the screens. The images were of Marcus' niece, and Shade was methodically transferring them to a secure cloud storage unit he had created.

The goal was straightforward: to erase her from the mainstream virtual realms, protecting her identity from prying eyes and potential threats. Marcus had emphasized the importance of keeping her involvement under wraps, and Shade was diligently ensuring that no trace of her digital footprint remained accessible to, well, anyone but him.

As he worked, one of the monitors previously switched off, whirred to life. But Shade's attention was singularly focused, his fingers tapping commands into the keyboard with mechanical precision, and so, he paid the anomaly no heed. It was only when the high-pitched beeping of a neglected device pulled him abruptly from his task. The sharp sound sliced through the ambient hum of computer fans and cooling systems, immediately commanding his attention.

The arcade machines around Shade flashed in the semi-darkness, their long-dormant screens sputtering to life with a flickering dance of colorful static. Cho lay sprawled on the floor, his limbs tangled in a nest of cables and wires. He remained oblivious, deep in a slumber. Shade turned swiftly towards the beeping device, his usually calm demeanor giving way to a growing sense of urgency.

His sharp eyes scanned the screen, which was now alive with a chaotic display of dialogue boxes, each screaming warnings about electrical overcharges and imminent failures.

"Dammit," Shade muttered under his breath, the realization of the unfolding catastrophe dawning on him like a thunderclap. The device in question was an exceptionally large CPU unit, its casing already beginning to emit thin tendrils of acrid smoke that curled upwards. The smoke's stench hit his nostrils, making him groan. He immediately recognized the criticality of the situation—the entire setup was on the brink of a catastrophic failure, something that could destroy a whole lot of progress.

Without a moment's hesitation, Shade lunged towards the CPU, his fingers dancing over the keys in a desperate attempt to override the system's fail-safes. But before he could even initiate the shutdown protocols, a powerful beam of current surged through the machine. It was as though the room itself had become possessed by an electrical storm. The current spread like wildfire, leaping across wires and cables, lighting up every nook and cranny of the cramped space with a pulsating glow. The makeshift workbenches, crafted from defunct arcade machines, groaned to life, their once silent circuits now singing with a haunting electronic choir.

The lights overhead blazed with an unnatural intensity, casting long, twisting shadows that writhed across the walls. The fan, mounted haphazardly on the wall, spun with furious energy, its blades slicing through the air with a whirring sound that seemed to forewarn of impending disaster. Shade's heart raced in sync with the escalating chaos around him. He knew he had to act fast; the system was spiraling out of control, and if he didn't find a way to contain the surge, it could spell ruin not just for his operation but might even set the whole place on fire.

Realizing the futility of continuing to manage the situation alone, he turned his attention to waking his companion.

"Get up, you donkey!" Shade shouted, urgency tinging his voice as he shook Cho's shoulder violently with one hand, the other hand bracing himself against the desk as the room trembled from the electric overcharge. "It's gonna blow!"

Cho's eyes snapped open, and he groggily looked around, unable to instantly understand what was happening. Just as his eyes focused on Shade…or rather above him, he let out a horrified yell.

And then, as abruptly as it had started, everything ceased. A deafening silence enveloped the room, and they were plunged into an oppressive darkness that seemed to swallow all sound and light. The only remnants of the frenzy were the faint wisps of smoke that hung in the air, the sharp scent of burnt circuits still lingering. Shade stood still, propping Cho up to his feet, unsure of why he had just yelled. In the quiet that followed, the ticking of cooling metal and the soft patter of settling dust were the only sounds to accompany his thoughts.

"Did you see that?" Cho mumbled, gripping his arm with a strength that could've broken it.

"See wha-"

Without warning, the very wires that snaked through the room began to twitch and thump with a life of their own. A low, vibrating hum resonated through the floor as if the entire room was beginning to stir under an unseen force. Shade could feel the charge building up around them, the air practically humming with static electricity.

Suddenly, arcs of electric blue light danced across the wires, illuminating the space with a ghastly glow. It was as if the energy itself was coalescing into something tangible, something alive.

Out of the tangled mess of wires and cables, a shape began to emerge, slowly taking form like a malicious specter born of pure electrical energy. It was an abomination—a creature forged from twisting muscle and crackling current, its form pulsating with an unnatural vitality. Its eyes were dark pits, voids in which crackled streaks of light swirled and danced. It stood before them, towering and sinuous, its body shifting with the fluidity of liquid lightning. From its limbs hung long, muscly vines that sparked and crackled, each one a conduit for the electric fury contained within.

Shade's heart pounded as he took an involuntary step back, his mind working to devise a plan. His earlier confidence was replaced with a deep-seated fear—a terror that came from facing something far beyond the scope of human comprehension.

To his side, Cho stood in utter disbelief, his eyes wide as he took in the creature's terrifying presence. The two men were pinned under its scrutiny, its gaze like an unblinking eye watching from the abyss.

With a flicker of motion, the creature unleashed a beam of searing light, a spear of electrical energy that shot across the room with blinding speed. It struck with a deafening crack, sending a cascade of sparks raining down like fiery stars.

Shade barely had time to react, instincts kicking in as he threw himself to the floor, narrowly evading the lethal arc. The beam carved a searing path through the room, leaving a smoldering trail in its wake. Cho, too, managed to dive clear, though his heart was still pounding with the knowledge that they were far out of their depth. Neither man was trained for a confrontation of this nature, and the realization was a bitter reminder of their own vulnerability.

As they scrambled to their feet, the creature's tendrils lashed out, moving with the grace of serpents seeking their prey. The cables that had been strewn haphazardly across the floor began to animate, each one coiling and uncoiling like mechanical vipers. The creature had assumed command of the wires, turning them into deadly extensions of its will.

The cables slithered across the floor with a mind of their own, each one driven by the creature's malevolent intent. Shade and Cho could see the electric charge surging through them, a deadly energy that promised certain death should it make contact.

"Move!" Shade shouted, his voice raw as he darted to the side, narrowly avoiding a whip-like lash of an electrified cable.

Cho stumbled forward, his body propelled by sheer adrenaline as he followed Shade's lead. The two men moved frantically, trying to stay one step ahead of the deadly tendrils that snapped and crackled with electric fury. In a split-second decision, Shade grabbed a nearby chair and flung it toward the creature, hoping to distract it even for a moment. The chairs collided with one of the tendrils, and the resulting discharge of energy sent wooden shards exploding in all directions, showering the room with debris.

Yet the creature remained unfazed, its dark eyes fixed on them with an unyielding determination. It hissed—a sound that resonated like the crackle of electricity, a low, threatening warning that filled the air with tension. The cables continued their pursuit, each one poised to strike. Shade and Cho dodged and ducked, their movements a frantic dance as they evaded the lethal lashings by mere inches. But it was clear they couldn't keep this up for long. The creature was ruthless, its attacks becoming increasingly coordinated as it closed in on them.

Just when they thought they might have a moment to regroup, a new threat emerged from the cable junction on the floor. Two smaller creatures materialized, formed from the same strange electrical energy that had birthed the first. These new arrivals were diminutive in size but no less intimidating. They moved with a swift, predatory grace, their bodies darting across the floor like lightning-given form.

Cho let out a strangled scream as one of the smaller creatures lunged toward him, its tendrils reaching out to zap him. He stumbled backward, tripping over his own feet as he fought to maintain balance. Shade realized they were cornered, caught between the looming threat of the larger creature and the ferocious onslaught of its smaller kin. His mind raced for a solution, for anything that might give them a fighting chance. The room was a mess of wires and makeshift furniture, every corner fraught with danger. Shade's gaze flicked to the array of arcade machines, and a desperate idea sparked in his mind.

"Cho, over here!" Shade shouted, signaling to the far side of the room where the old machines stood silent and foreboding. Cho understood immediately, his eyes widening with a mix of hope and desperation. Together, they made a mad dash toward the machines, ducking and weaving through the onslaught of cables that sought to ensnare them. Shade reached the machines first, his hands moving with practiced speed as he began to manipulate the old circuits and wiring. The arcade machines had been a part of his operation for years, repurposed into workstations and now their potential saviors.

In a flurry of motion, Shade managed to rig the machines to serve as an impromptu barrier, a tangled mess of metal and wires that offered them some semblance of protection. The cables hissed and sparked as they struck against the machines, their energy dissipating harmlessly into the metal casings. It was a temporary solution, but it bought them precious time. The creatures continued to circle, probing for weaknesses. The duo crouched behind their makeshift shield, breathing heavily as they tried to catch their breath. The adrenaline was still coursing through their veins, their minds sharp and focused despite the chaos around them.

"We can't hold out like this forever," Cho panted, his eyes flicking between the creatures and their dwindling cover.

"I know," Shade replied, his voice grim but determined. "But we need to find a way to take these things down."

With the creature's harsh assault showing no signs of abating, Shade knew they had to act fast. The arcade machines would only hold for so long, and once their protection failed, they would be at the mercy of the creature's deadly power.

At that moment, Shade made a decision. He remembered something like that from an old cartoon he had once watched as a kid.

"When I say so, make a run for it," Shade instructed, his mind working rapidly to piece together a plan.

Cho looked at him incredulously, but he nodded, trusting Shade's judgment despite the overwhelming odds stacked against them.

With a deep breath, Shade prepared to execute his gambit. He reached for the exposed wires, his fingers dancing over the circuits as he rerouted the current, channeling the excess energy into the surrounding equipment. The room was a veritable minefield of electrical hazards, and Shade intended to make the most of it. He could feel the energy surging through the machines, a crackling buildup of power that would soon be unleashed.

"Now, Cho!" Shade yelled, his voice cutting through the chaos.

Cho didn't hesitate. He sprang from their cover, sprinting toward the door with all the speed he could muster, hoping to draw the creature's attention away from Shade's preparations. As he made his desperate run, Shade completed the final adjustments, feeling the circuits hum with lethal potential. With a final twist of the wires, he unleashed the energy, sending a cascading wave of electric force rippling through the room. The resulting explosion of light and sound was blinding, a brilliant detonation that consumed the space in a dazzling hellhole. The creatures were caught in the blast, their forms writhing and convulsing as the energy coursed through them, tearing them apart from within.

When the light finally faded and the echoes of the explosion dissipated, Shade stood amidst the wreckage, his chest heaving with exertion. The air was thick with the smell of ozone and burnt metal.

The creatures lay defeated, their forms dissolving into wisps of smoke and fading embers. The cables that had once moved with deadly purpose were now inert, lifeless strands strewn across the floor.

Cho approached cautiously, his eyes wide at what they had just survived. "That was... insane," he mumbled.

With the immediate threat neutralized, the duo set to work, sifting through the wreckage for any equipment that might have survived the wreckage. The mystery of the LHC was growing ever deeper, and while Shade had initially dismissed the indications of 'interdimensional' breakage, he was willing to believe just a little.

* * *

Meanwhile, back at Dr. Shaw's humble family home, Marcus Flynn sat at the dining table as he tried to think of ways to confront the Cabal. Harrows was a seasoned military veteran and could probably call in favors if he wanted to. Just as he was busy thinking of what to get Shade and Phoenix to do next, his phone buzzed on the table next to his hand, snapping him out of his focused trance. The notification was from an encrypted messaging app he used to communicate with Phoenix. As he opened the message, his eyes widened.

>Phoenix:

Alert: Major electrical surge detected at Containment Unit 07. Situation similar to LHC. Possible breach in security protocols. Urgent attention needed.

Marcus felt a knot form in his stomach. The Containment Unit housed the entity they had captured—a creature born from the anomalies at the LHC. He had yet to see the destructive potential of these anomalies firsthand but knew that any breach could spell disaster.

His fingers hesitated over the keypad as he quickly typed a response, seeking more information.

>BigRedStud

What exactly is happening? I'm away from the facility with Harrows. Need specifics to inform Dr. Shaw.

>Phoenix:

Initial assessment shows containment compromised. The entity's pod is cracked open. There's no one inside the room right now.

Marcus exhaled sharply, relieved that at least no personnel were inside the containment unit when the breach occurred. He immediately reached for his phone and called Dr. Evelyn Shaw. As the line rang, he couldn't shake the uneasy feeling growing in his gut.

"Doctor," Marcus said the moment he picked up, his voice urgent, "we have a situation. Phoenix just alerted me to a rupture in Containment Unit 07. The entity's pod is compromised, and it's trying to escape. Are you at the facility?"

"I'm on my way," Dr. Shaw responded. "I'll have the team initiate lockdown procedures and get to the control room immediately."

"Good. Keep me updated. I'll coordinate with Phoenix on any developments," Marcus assured her before hanging up.

He was about to relay more information to Phoenix when his phone buzzed again.

>Phoenix:

Ayoub is heading toward the Containment Unit. Access code has been entered.

Marcus' heart skipped a beat. Nadia, his niece, was about to walk into a potential death trap.

"Damn it," he muttered under his breath, feeling a cold sweat break across his forehead. His mind was a whirlwind of possibilities, each one worse than the last. He couldn't let anything happen to one of his own. She was like a daughter to him.

He immediately typed a frantic message to Phoenix.

>BigRedStud

Get me a live feed from the Containment Unit. I need eyes on that room now!

Seconds ticked by agonizingly slow as he waited for a response. Finally, the encrypted messaging app dinged with an incoming link. He clicked it without hesitation, bringing up a grainy but live video feed from inside the containment chamber on his laptop screen.

The video showed the interior of Containment Unit 07, eerily silent and dimly lit by the red emergency lights that cast long, unsettling shadows. Sparks of electricity flickered intermittently around the pod, which was clearly damaged, its once-sealed surface now sporting a web of fractures.

Marcus leaned in closer, his eyes scanning the room for any sign of the creature. The feed captured an unnerving emptiness—until the camera shifted slightly, and he caught a glimpse of movement.

There, creeping along the far wall, was the entity. It was a twisted amalgamation of muscle and energy, a horrifying testament to the unnatural forces unleashed by the LHC's anomalies. Its elongated limbs moved with grace, each step deliberate as it explored its newfound freedom.

Marcus watched, horrified, as the creature slowly turned its attention toward the main entrance, where Nadia would soon appear if she wasn't stopped. He frantically pulled out his phone, dialing Nadia's number with trembling fingers.

"Come on, pick up," he urged quietly, the ringing tone echoing in his ears like a countdown ticking toward disaster.

The call went unanswered, heightening his sense of urgency. He had no choice but to try another tactic. Quickly switching to the messaging app, he shot off a desperate text to Phoenix, hoping they could intervene in time.

>BigRedStud

She's about to enter the unit. Can you override the door controls? We need to keep her out!

>Phoenix

Proceeding.

Finally, the door to the containment unit began to open, its mechanical whir echoing through the speakers. Marcus' breath caught in his throat as the feed revealed Nadia stepping into the frame. She stood a step behind the doorway, momentarily frozen by the unexpected sight of the creature now focused entirely on her. Its head tilted as if sensing her presence, its jagged, twisted form framed by the crimson light that bathed the chamber. Marcus, feeling utterly powerless, could only watch through the screen. As the creature shifted, its body tensing like a predator about to pounce, Nadia finally seemed to sense the imminent threat. Her eyes widened in alarm as she took in the creature's nasty form.

He saw her lips move but had no idea about what she could've said because it made the entity leap towards her.

"Outta there, lass!" Marcus shouted at his screen, wishing desperately that she could hear him.

But before the creature could touch her, Phoenix's efforts finally paid off. The door in front of Nadia slid shut with a resounding clang, locking her out of the containment chamber and sealing the creature within once more.

Marcus let out a breath, relief flooding through him. He immediately sent another message to Phoenix, expressing his gratitude while also ensuring the situation was contained.

>BigRedStud

Thank you. I can't say it enough times.

>Phoenix:

No worries. Resuming surveillance.

With the immediate crisis averted, Marcus knew they had to act fast to prevent further breaches. He quickly composed another message, this time directed to Dr. Shaw, informing her of the situation and ensuring she was aware of the steps needed to reinforce the containment protocols.

As he sat back in his chair, the weight of the situation settled heavily on his shoulders. The LHC's anomalies and the entity were both far more unpredictable than any of them had anticipated. He glanced at the live feed one more time, the creature now restless within its confines. He knew that despite their numbers, they were still at a disadvantage unless they kept learning with each encounter. Only then they might just have a chance against this nightmare.

Just as he was about to lean back and thank God for not having a heart attack, his phone buzzed. An unknown foreign number was displayed on the screen as he accepted the call.

"Flynn," the voice on the other end breathed amongst the patter of rain in the background, "Shade speaking…we've got a situation."

Chapter 5: Cult of the New Dawn

Times Square, New York, USA

The bright lights of Times Square were drowned out by the sheer number of people gathered there. The usually bustling and chaotic atmosphere had given way to an eerie uniformity. Rows upon rows of individuals clad in black and crimson robes marched through the heart of New York City, their faces hidden behind intricate masks depicting a mix of ancient symbols and futuristic designs.

A massive banner unfurled above the crowd, bearing the ominous slogan: *"Through Science, We Have Found Our Gods."*

Chants echoed off the surrounding skyscrapers, a sinister blend of harmony and discord that captivated and unnerved the tourists and locals who stopped to watch.

"We've touched the fabric of reality!" they cried, "The age of the new gods is upon us!"

Their march was orchestrated with military precision. Each step seemed to resonate with the beats of a thousand drums, and their voices combined into a cacophony that reverberated throughout Times Square.

The Cabal's followers carried illuminated symbols reminiscent of ancient sigils but interwoven with mathematical equations and DNA sequences. Each held a staff tipped with a crystal that pulsed with a strange, hypnotic light.

"Join us, brothers and sisters," a voice amplified through loudspeakers called out, "In embracing the truth of our evolution!"

Their presence dominated the area, driving the usual chaos of Times Square into an unsettling silence, as though the very heart of the city paused to acknowledge the spectacle unfolding.

Pearl Harbor, Hawaii, USA

The peace of Pearl Harbor was shattered by the rhythmic chants of the Cabal's followers. In contrast to the serene waters and historical reverence of the place, the followers stood defiantly in long lines along the coastline, their robes billowing in the gentle sea breeze.

"Through destruction, we have forged new pathways!" their leader intoned, standing atop a makeshift platform. "From the ashes of the past, the gods shall rise again!"

Behind them, the imposing silhouette of the USS Arizona Memorial stood as a silent witness to this eerie congregation. The contrast was stark—here, where thousands had given their lives, a new order proclaimed itself as the harbinger of the future.

The followers held torches that emitted an unnatural, flickering blue light, casting eerie shadows that danced across the historic site.

"History is but the gateway to our ascension!" they shouted in unison, eyes alight with fanaticism.

London Bridge, London, United Kingdom

Under the grey skies of London, the Cabal's followers paraded across the iconic London Bridge, their numbers swelling like a dark tide against the backdrop of the Thames. The sound of their chanting rose above the murmur of the river, drowning out the sounds of the city.

"London, hear us!" their leader called out, her voice echoing with an ethereal cadence. "We stand on the threshold of a new dawn!"

The people of London watched from a distance, some taking photos, others simply staring in shock and confusion at the spectacle. Police were on standby, observing but keeping a safe distance; their faces were a mix of apprehension and disbelief.

"Embrace the science that unveils the divine," the crowd chanted, moving in unison like a singular, sentient entity. "Join us as we usher in an era beyond the constraints of your mortal understanding!"

The Great Pyramids, Giza, Egypt

In the shadow of the ancient pyramids, the Cabal's followers marched with a reverence that seemed almost sacrilegious. The sands of Giza swirled around them as they processed, their footsteps forming a path through millennia of history. Somewhere in the distance, the *Azaan* called out, but the call to something holy was drowned under the pleas of the ever-persistent darkness.

"Behold the wonders of the ancients!" their leader proclaimed, gesturing towards the towering structures. "Science has resurrected their knowledge, and with it, we ascend!"

The pyramids loomed behind them, timeless and imposing, as the followers unfurled a banner that bore hieroglyphs interspersed with modern symbols of science—a juxtaposition that defied tradition.

"From the sands of time, we emerge anew!" they chanted, each voice carrying the weight of conviction, each step echoing with the echoes of eternity.

The spectacle was watched by tourists and locals alike, many of whom stood in stunned silence while others captured the moment on their phones, sending the images out into the world.

Fountains of Shalimar Gardens, Lahore, Pakistan

The lush greenery and serene waters of the Shalimar Gardens became the unlikely stage for the Cabal's followers, their black and crimson robes contrasting sharply against the vibrant backdrop. The scent of flowers mingled with the strange, electric energy that seemed to emanate from their ranks.

"In the cradle of civilization, we bring forth the dawn of a new era!" their leader declared, arms outstretched towards the cascading waters of the fountains. "In the name of the Great Civilization that once walked the same marshes, we have found a way to make the gods speak!"

The Cabal's presence felt both alien and natural, as though they were reclaiming a forgotten legacy buried within the earth itself.

"We stand united in our quest for enlightenment!" they proclaimed, their voices rising and falling like the fountains themselves. "Like those who came before us and those who will after us!"

The followers formed a circle around the central fountain; their eyes closed in collective meditation as they continued to chant, their words a harmonious blend of prayer and prophecy.

Streets of Seine, Paris, France

The historic streets along the Seine in Paris were alive with the sound of the Cabal's march. The air was thick with the scent of revolution, reminiscent of a time when the city had been the epicenter of upheaval and change.

"From birth to rebirth!" their leader's voice carried over the cobblestones. "Join us as we uncover the mysteries of the universe!"

Their procession moved with fluid grace, a river of robes flowing along the banks of the Seine. The Cabal's followers raised their hands to the sky as though drawing power from the ancient city itself.

The people of Paris watched with a mixture of fascination and fear, unsure of what to make of this unprecedented demonstration that blended science with something far more sinister.

Kyoto, Tokyo, Japan

In Kyoto, where tradition and modernity coexist in a delicate balance, the Cabal's followers made their presence known with a surreal elegance. The tranquil beauty of the cherry blossoms provided the contrast to their dark energy which seemed to emanate from their procession.

"Walk with us!" their leader announced, their voice resonating with an almost supernatural clarity. "The kami of the wires speaks more truth than the ones above!"

The followers moved silently through the streets, their footsteps barely audible against the soft rustle of leaves. They carried lanterns that flickered with an otherworldly light, casting shadows that danced like specters against the ancient architecture. The people of Kyoto watched with quiet awe, their expressions a mix of curiosity and caution as the Cabal's followers wove their way through the historic city.

Mount Ararat, Ararat, Turkey

In the ancient city of Istanbul, where east meets west, the Cabal's followers marched with a purpose that seemed to transcend time itself. The city's rich history served as a backdrop for their enigmatic procession, a tapestry of cultures woven together into a singular entity.

"Ararat, the birthplace of mankind's five Adams!" their leader proclaimed, arms raised in invocation. "Join us as we unlock the secrets of the cosmos!"

Their voices echoed off the terraces, creating a haunting symphony that resonated with an ancient power. The followers carried banners adorned with symbols that merged ancient alchemy with cutting-edge science, a testament to their belief in a new order.

"In unity, we transcend the boundaries of existence! Defy the floods that once sought to destroy us!" they chanted, their voices a chorus of unwavering faith.

Tao Dan Park, Ho Chi Minh City, Vietnam

In the vibrant streets of Vietnam, the Cabal's followers marched with a fervor that matched the pulsating energy of the city. The air was thick with the scent of incense and the rhythm of drums, creating an atmosphere charged with anticipation.

"Fear not, O' cradle of resilience!" their leader intoned, his voice a beacon of certainty. "We are the heralds of a new dawn!"

Their procession was a spectacle of sound and color, a mesmerizing blend of tradition and modernity that captivated all who bore witness. The followers moved with fluid grace, their robes billowing like shadows against the backdrop of the city's skyline. The people of Vietnam watched with a mixture of awe and trepidation, unsure of what to make of this enigmatic demonstration that seemed to defy logic and reason.

As the world watched this unprecedented demonstration unfold, Marcus Flynn and John Harrows sat on the floral couch, eyes fixed on the live broadcast being transmitted across the globe.

"This isn't just a demonstration," Harrows said, his voice tinged with apprehension. "It's a declaration of war against the status quo."

Marcus nodded, aware that The Cabal's actions were a catalyst, a spark that threatened to ignite a global upheaval unlike anything the world had ever seen.

"They're playing a dangerous game, mate," Marcus replied, his voice low and steady. "And we're all caught in the crossfire."

The television continued to broadcast the Cabal's march, each image a testament to the power and reach of their movement. For Marcus and Harrows, the stakes had never been higher, and the path ahead was fraught with uncertainty and peril.

"We need to act," Harrows looked perplexed. "Before it's too late."

Marcus hummed in agreement, his mind already working on a plan. The world was changing, and they had a role to play in shaping their destiny—a destiny that hung precariously in the balance.

* * *

Thomas Anderson sprinted through the brightly lit corridors of the facility, his heart pounding in his chest. The rhythmic sound of his footsteps echoed off the cold, white walls as he weaved past startled employees who could sense the urgency in his demeanor. He held his phone tightly, the screen displaying the global broadcast of the Cabal's massive demonstration.

As he approached the expansive lobby, Thomas could already hear the low murmur of voices mingling with the unmistakable sound of the broadcast. He burst through the doors, coming to a halt as he surveyed the room. The lobby was a sea of faces, all turned towards the enormous screen that dominated one wall. The screen flickered with scenes of the Cabal's followers marching through cities worldwide, their message resonating across continents. Thomas pushed his way through the crowd, his eyes scanning for one person in particular: Jeremiah Smith.

There, at the front of the room, stood Jeremiah. His usually composed attitude was replaced by an expression of wide-eyed astonishment as he watched the unfolding events on the screen. Around him, facility workers exchanged hushed whispers, their faces reflecting a mixture of fear, curiosity, and disbelief. They stood motionless, gaze locked on the screen. The camera feed shifted from one city to another, showcasing the sheer scale and coordination of the Cabal's demonstration.

"Jesus," Jeremiah muttered under his breath, his voice barely audible over the broadcast.

The scene cut to the followers in Kyoto, their eerie chanting rising above the tranquil backdrop of cherry blossoms. The juxtaposition of beauty and menace was palpable, and the crowd watching in the lobby shifted uneasily.

Thomas finally reached Jeremiah's side, out of breath but driven by urgency. "Jeremiah," he shook his head. "This is bad."

Jeremiah's mind raced as he tried to comprehend the implications of what he was witnessing. The Cabal was not just a local phenomenon; it was a global movement, one that threatened to reshape the very fabric of society.

"I... I knew they were growing," Thomas said, more to himself than to Jeremiah. "Because people would talk about it on internet channels, but this…this is unprecedented."

The other nodded, his eyes flicking between the young man and the screen. The weight of the situation was settling in, a heavy burden that threatened to squeeze the air out of their lungs.

＊ ＊ ＊

In a crowded New York City subway station, commuters stopped in their tracks, their eyes drawn to the screens usually reserved for advertisements. The Cabal's procession in Times Square played out in real-time, and the passengers watched with undefinable emotions.

Some were intrigued, their faces lit with a curiosity that bordered on fascination. Others were visibly frightened, the implications of the Cabal's words echoing in their minds. A few looked enraged, their fists clenched as they muttered under their breath about the audacity of such a public display.

An older woman clutched her shopping bags tightly, her eyes wide with apprehension as she turned to the man beside her.

"Those Devil worshipers!" her frail, wrinkly face burned pink with disdain.

Across the Atlantic, in Europe, similar scenes played out. In France, Parisian streets were bustling, but an air of unease lingered. News outlets displayed footage of marches, their participants draped in the dark robes of the Cabal, their faces obscured but their voices loud and clear. In cities like London and Berlin, where the contrast between the old world and new ideologies often clashed, the atmosphere was thick with debate and skepticism. Military aircraft had begun to soar the skies, patrolling for any signs of extreme unrest.

In Berlin, a group of concerned citizens gathered outside the Reichstag building, their voices a harmonious blend of concern and defiance. The Cabal's presence was felt everywhere, sparking conversations that ranged from philosophical to fearful.

Meanwhile, in a less-than-respectable pub nestled in some smelly London hole, patrons gathered around the television mounted above the bar. The usual chatter and clinking of glasses had fallen silent, replaced by the somber cadence of the Cabal's chanting as they marched across London Bridge.

A young man, his pint forgotten on the counter, leaned forward with interest.

"Bloody hell, they're everywhere," he shook the other older man up from his drunken midday slumber. "This ain't just some local cult."

His friend groaned, rubbing his temples. "Mate, they're just havin' a laugh, pulling yer leg. Nothin' to worry 'bout."

Elsewhere, in a cozy Italian café, the television set in the corner flickered with images of the Cabal's procession along the Pisa. Diners paused mid-bite, their attention captured by the spectacle unfolding on the screen.

A middle-aged man whispered to his wife, his voice full of fear and disbelief. "Hope there won't be rats to eat this time…"

His wife, sipping her coffee with a steady hand, nodded slowly. "Can't bear to hear about the Tower burning again."

Asian cities like Ikebukuro and Hong Kong found themselves caught in a whirlwind of speculation and intrigue. Ikebukuro's neon-lit streets, usually a symbol of relentless energy and progress, seemed overshadowed by the weight of the world's unrest. Crowds gathered around public screens, watching the broadcasts that detailed the escalating situation. Hong Kong saw its own share of turmoil. People watched from their homes and workplaces, engaging in fervent discussions about the Cabal and the implications of their claims about science leading to gods.

Somewhere on the bustling streets of Tokyo, large digital billboards broadcasted the Cabal's march in Shanghai. Passersby stopped to watch, their expressions ranging from mild curiosity to outright fear. The city's usual frenetic pace slowed as people absorbed the gravity of what was happening.

A group of teenagers stood in awe, their eyes fixed on the screen. "This is crazy," one of them said, snapping a picture with his phone. "It's like something out of a movie."

In the Middle East, the vibrant streets of Cairo and Abu Dhabi buzzed with conversation as residents speculated about the implications of the Cabal's rise. The media, a powerful tool for both information and propaganda, played a significant role in shaping perceptions.

All the while, in the colorful markets of Marrakesh, vendors paused in their work, their eyes fixed on screens displaying the latest developments. Conversations flowed, interweaving concerns with curiosity about the global events unfolding before them. And in remote African villages, where news traveled at a slower pace, communities huddled around radios, listening intently to broadcasts that painted a picture of unrest far beyond their borders.

In general, there were those who were enraged, their anger stoked by the Cabal's brazen actions and the perceived threat to their way of life. And yet, there were also those exhilarated by the prospect of change, seeing in the chaos a chance for new beginnings and the possibility of untapped potential.

Back at the New Dawn facility's lobby, the tension was palpable. The room was filled with employees exchanging worried glances as they watched the unfolding events on the screen.

At that moment, both Jeremiah and Thomas understood that the world was on the brink of transformation, and the Cabal stood to reshape the future in ways that were both thrilling and terrifying. As the broadcast continued to play out on screens across the world, one thing was clear: the world would never be the same again.

* * *

At a cramped, bustling Manila internet café, the air was filled with the hum of outdated computers and the frenetic tapping of keyboards. The scent of fried food fused with the pungent smell of sweat permeated the small room, which was packed with patrons absorbed in their digital worlds.

Shade and Cho were seated at a corner booth, a makeshift workstation cluttered with cables and devices. Shade, his eyes bloodshot from lack of sleep, stared at the screen, fingers flying over the keyboard as he clicked through encrypted data files. Cho, reclining in his chair with one leg propped up on the table, idly scrolled through social media feeds on his laptop, looking for any mention of their recent escapades.

Shade rubbed his temple, trying to dispel the fog of exhaustion that clouded his mind. He hadn't slept properly for days, the weight of Marcus's requests and the pressure of keeping an eye on the LHC facility wearing on him. Suddenly, the door swung open with a creak, and a man burst into the café, panting heavily as he looked around with wide eyes. He quickly spotted a friend seated at one of the computers and rushed over, speaking in rapid and excited Tagalog.

"Have you heard?" the newcomer exclaimed, his voice rising above the general din of the café. "It's amazing what they show on TV! The Cabals are there; they're all over the world!"

The patron he addressed looked up, intrigued. He gestured for the newcomer to pull up a chair, and together, they opened a browser window, navigating to the live broadcast that had captured global attention.

Shade, half-listening to the commotion, picked up snippets of the conversation, his fluency in Tagalog allowing him to grasp the urgency of the situation. Cho, ever the opportunist, leaned over and opened the broadcast on his laptop, curiosity piqued by the excitement buzzing around the room.

The screen flickered to life, displaying the chilling footage of the Cabal's march across the world. Dressed in their distinctive black robes, the Cabal's followers moved through iconic landmarks with an unsettling sense of purpose. Their chants, a haunting blend of Scientology's clinical detachment and Satanism's dark fervor, echoed ominously through the streets of each city.

Shade, shifting his attention back to his own screen, mumbled under his breath in English, "Looks like the Cabal's gone global. Typical."

His tone was laced with disdain, his fingers continuing to tap rhythmically on the keyboard as he resumed his work. Cho glanced at him, a smirk playing on his lips. "So, are we supposed to be scared now?" he asked sarcastically, casually leaning back in his chair, belying the tension in the room.

Shade shook his head, a faint smile tugging at the corners of his mouth. "Neh, not really? We've got other things to worry about."

He gestured to the collection of digital files displayed on his monitor, their contents a jumble of codes and schematics that only he could decipher. "I've recovered the data," Shade said, his voice low but confident. "But we can't stay here forever. Flynn was supposed to arrange something for us."

Cho nodded, slightly frustrated as he glanced around the cramped café. "Yeah, I know. We can't just be sitting here in this café with a setup like this."

The noise of the café seemed to grow louder, the buzz of conversations blending with the rhythmic clatter of keyboards. Shade leaned back in his chair, rubbing his eyes as he tried to shake off the fatigue that was almost overwhelming.

"He had better come through soon," Shade mumbled, almost to himself.

As the Cabal's broadcast continued to play out across the globe, Shade and Cho remained rooted in their seats. Despite the chaos unfolding on the screen, they were unfazed, their focus firmly fixed on the task at hand.

* * *

Harrows paced restlessly across the living room of Dr. Shaw's old family house, its vintage charm offering some homely comfort against the urgent situation unfolding around the world. The room was a mixture of the old and new; aged wooden beams crossed the ceiling, and shelves lined with dusty books hinted at the home's history, while the large, flat-screen TV displayed a muted broadcast of the Cabal's followers marching. Marcus sat nearby, his laptop open on the antique coffee table, the glow from the screen highlighting the furrow in his brow as he scanned through the news feeds and messages coming in.

The late morning air outside was still and quiet, a deceptive calm that opposed the madness sweeping across nations. The Cabal's march and the reports of global unrest had ignited a sense of urgency within them both. Harrows and Marcus knew they needed more than just the information they had—they needed insight from someone who could provide a military perspective on the brewing chaos.

Harrows, a man of robust build and military bearing, paused by the window, the light from a nearby lamp casting his profile in sharp relief. He rubbed his chin thoughtfully, the grizzled texture of his beard catching the light as he considered his options. Then, reaching a decision, he turned back to Marcus.

"I'm going to call an old friend," Harrows' voice, despite its usual booming nature, had a slight tremor in it. "We need to see this situation from a military angle, and there's no one better than Major Samuel Whitmore. We've been through a lot together. I'm sure he can give us the lowdown on what's really happening out there."

Marcus nodded, his fingers curling against his cigarette as he continued his scroll for updates on his phone. "Good idea. We need all the intel we can get. This thing is spiraling out of control fast."

Harrows did not need any more affirmation. He dialed the number from memory, each ring on the line heightening the anticipation. When Whitmore's voice finally came through, deep and steady, it was like hearing a lifeline through the noise of the storm.

"Sam," Harrows greeted, his tone warm despite the tension. "It's Jack. I know it's been a while, but I need a favor."

There was a pause, then a slight chuckle from Whitmore. "Harrows, as I live and breathe. What's this about? You sound like you're knee-deep in something big. Don't tell me you've gotten tangled up in this shitshow."

Harrows took a deep breath, bracing himself. "We've got uprisings and violent outbursts all across the States. The Cabal is on the move, and I need to know what the military's doing about it. We're seeing states like South Carolina, Illinois, Minnesota, and North Dakota getting hit hard."

Whitmore's tone shifted, a seriousness settling in as he replied. "You're not wrong. Things *are* dicey out here. The military's spread thin, trying to manage the bullshit. We've got organized marches turning into riots. It's a damn mess. But it'll heal, they go back in after a few hours."

Harrows exchanged a look with Marcus, who was listening intently. This was the confirmation they needed—things were escalating faster than they'd anticipated.

"North Dakota is a particular concern," Harrows continued, trying to convey the urgency without revealing too much about their proximity to the New Dawn facility. "I've got a plan that might help contain this before it gets any worse. But I need someone who can see the bigger picture, someone like you who understands the stakes."

On the other end, Whitmore's silence was thoughtful, considering the weight of Harrows' request. The connection crackled slightly.

"What exactly are you proposing, Jack?" Whitmore finally asked, the directness of his question underlined by a readiness to act.

Harrows leaned against the window frame, the city lights outside casting a gentle glow through the curtains. "I'm talking about a rogue mission, Sam. I need your expertise and your team to help stabilize this situation. We might have to bend some rules to prevent a full-scale catastrophe."

Whitmore exhaled sharply, the sound of his resolve coming through the line. "You do realize what you're asking, right? If this goes south, we could all be looking at some serious consequences."

Harrows nodded, knowing full well the risks involved. "I understand, Sam. But if we don't act now, we might not have a chance later. I need someone who can provide the necessary arrangements, someone who can help us get a handle on this."

The silence stretched out again, and Harrows could almost hear the gears turning in Whitmore's mind. Finally, the major spoke, his voice filled with the assurance of a man who had faced similar battles before.

"Alright, Harrows. I'll get a team on this. They'll be in plain clothes, nothing that'll draw attention, but they're some of the best we have. You make sure you're ready when they arrive and keep me in the loop. We'll get through this."

As the call ended, he turned to Marcus, who had been listening to the one-sided conversation with a keen interest.

"We've got support coming," Harrows informed him, his voice carrying a newfound confidence. "Whitmore's sending a team. We'll need to be ready for them and coordinate our next steps carefully."

Marcus nodded, placing his phone on the armrest of the couch and leaning back, a thoughtful expression on his face. "Good. We're going to need all the help we can get. The world's on the edge, and we're sitting at the center of it."

\>Reaper

Phoenix. We've got a situation. You need to lay low. The government's cracking down—severing links, maybe even prepping for lockdown procedures. It's about public safety. Things could escalate fast. Be ready to drop off the grid if necessary.

He paused for a moment, considering the implications of what he was asking. Phoenix was invaluable, a digital ghost weaving through the complex web of global data. If they were forced into hiding, their access to critical information would be severely limited.

But Harrows knew it was a necessary precaution. The government was moving swiftly to contain the unrest, and anyone with ties to the core of the Cabal's exposure could easily become a target. There was an old maid's tale that he often heard during his tour in Afghanistan.

'They shoot first and ask the questions later.'

The last thing he needed was for someone who was the sole reason for his survival in his mission to have to lose their life due to an intense situation.

He hit send and watched as the message encrypted itself, a barrier against prying eyes. Marcus glanced up from his phone, sensing the tension in Harrows' demeanor.

"You good, big guy?" A plume of smoke left Marcus' lips and nostrils as he exhaled.

"I've just warned Phoenix to keep their head down," Harrows replied, leaning back in his chair with a heavy sigh. "The government's tightening its grip. They're severing communications, probably gearing up for something big. They might enforce lockdowns soon."

Marcus nodded, understanding the stakes. "Makes sense. With the Cabal's followers marching and all the unrest, they're probably trying to control the narrative and prevent panic."

Meanwhile, at the motel room on the outskirts of Fargo, Zara Akhtar received Harrows' message. The soft glow of her laptop was the only light in the room, her fingers poised above the keyboard as she analyzed lines of code and reams of data scrolling across the screen. Her heart skipped a beat as she read Harrows' warning. The government's actions weren't entirely unexpected, but the reality of going dark was a bitter pill to swallow. She'd been close to uncovering more of the Cabal's secrets; their tendrils spread far and wide, touching governments, corporations, and private citizens alike.

Her fingers danced over the keyboard, crafting a response.

>Phoenix

Understood. I'll pull back and keep my activities minimal. But I'm close to something that might give us more leverage. I'll keep digging under the radar. Let me know if you find out anything specific.

She sent the message and breathed out slowly, glancing at the second screen that displayed security feeds and system logs from the LHC facility. The data stream was steady, but the undercurrents were chaotic—a digital battlefield she had become intimately familiar with.

Zara knew the risks of staying active. The Cabal's digital watchdogs were relentless, their algorithms designed to hunt down any perceived threats. But she also understood the stakes—her discoveries could potentially alter the course of what was unfolding worldwide.

❊ ❊ ❊

Washington D.C., USA
Tuesday 16 34

At the heart of the nation's governance, military personnel and law enforcement units were visibly bolstered. Streets that once thrummed with the daily ebb and flow of civilian life were now patrolled by uniformed guards, their presence a clear indication of the gravity of the situation. Public places, typically bustling with activity, saw fewer crowds as citizens were advised to stay indoors.

At the Pentagon, the nerve center of the U.S. defense strategy, high-ranking officials convened emergency meetings, poring over data and reports that painted a picture of civil unrest growing at an alarming rate. The Cabal's influence was spreading, sparking protests and violence in several key states. South Carolina, Illinois, Minnesota, and North Dakota stood out on the digital map, marked with bright red symbols indicating regions of heightened conflict.

In South Carolina, an otherwise serene neighborhood found itself disrupted by the angry roars of protestors, their chants echoing through the streets. The air was thick with tension, and the presence of military vehicles only served to amplify the unrest.

"It's like a powder keg out there," one of Harrows' military contacts had described in a secure call, his voice tense with concern. "The Cabal's managed to light a fire, and if we're not careful, it'll spread faster than we can handle. Major General Whitmore has instructed for special artillery from the NATO states. We will be bringing the equipment in if necessary."

Harrows nodded, his expression thoughtful but determined. Once the phone clicked off, he turned to look at Marcus, who had just been on the phone with Dr. Shaw. "We have to stay ahead, Marcus. The Cabal may have sparked this, but we can't let them dictate how it ends."

"Any idea what the weapons will be?" Marcus asked, massaging his temples with his fingers.

"Nano-tech suits from what I know. There are different firing and long-range weapons included, but I think they will work more as they test them out on captured entities." Harrows' reply was met with a sarcastic grin that made him roll his eyes.

"You're gonna wear tights, big guy?" he laughed.

"Stop being immature. It's armor," Harrows retorted, marching out in the backyard to check on Max.

Harrows knew that something was going to happen. It was a feeling deep in his gut that they would soon face something far worse than a cult. Some less breakable.

Less human.

* * *

The air in the Philippines was thick with humidity, the early morning sun casting long shadows through the bustling streets of Manila. Shade sat at a cramped table in the back of the internet cafe, his face illuminated by the bluish glow of the computer screen in front of him. He sipped a lukewarm cup of coffee mixed with whatever energy drink Cho had placed in front of him as he scrolled through lines of code, cross-referencing data streams that flickered with activity.

The atmosphere in the cafe was the usual, filled with the buzz of people going about their business, completely oblivious to the high-stakes drama unfolding halfway across the globe. The demonstrations had occurred hours ago, and for the people in these poverty-stricken areas, it had done little but provide a brief moment of entertainment. His phone buzzed against the wooden table, vibrating noisily. Shade grabbed it, checking the message from Marcus, his eyes narrowing as he read:

>BigRedStud

Get ready to move. Pack whatever you need and send me your current coordinates. I'll arrange for a pick-up.

Shade's thin lips curled into a half-smirk. He didn't need to be told twice. The message was cryptic enough to pique his interest yet clear in its urgency. There was something happening behind the scenes, something big, and Shade knew better than to question Marcus' instincts.

Cho, who had been absentmindedly browsing through random websites on a nearby terminal, noticed the change in Shade's demeanor and looked over. "What's up, man?" Cho asked, his tone casual but laced with curiosity.

"Time to go," Shade replied, downing the rest of his coffee in one swift gulp. "Marcus wants us out of here. We've got a ride coming."

Cho arched an eyebrow, his fingers pausing on the keyboard. "Where to?"

Shade shrugged nonchalantly. "He didn't say, but I hope it's somewhere cooler," Shade leaned back in his chair, pondering the message's implications. "You know how these things go. It's always on a need-to-know basis."

Shade quickly powered down the computers, yanking the cords free from their sockets. The hard drives he'd been using were wiped clean, their contents encrypted and stored in his cloud network—if anyone was determined enough to try and trace his activities, they'd find nothing but digital dust. He gestured for Cho to start packing up their gear, and the younger man nodded as he began gathering their things. Together, they worked efficiently, dismantling the makeshift setup they'd pieced together over the last few days. It was a testament to their skills that they could blend into the background so seamlessly, only leaving a trace if they intended to.

"Make sure you've got everything you need," Shade instructed, eyeing Cho's methodical packing. "We're not coming back here."

With their belongings packed, Shade moved to a quieter corner of the cafe and dialed Marcus. The connection buzzed, and then Marcus's voice came through, faint but clear amidst the static.

"Ready?" Marcus asked, skipping any pretense of small talk.

Shade replied, checking his watch. "Where are you sending us?"

Marcus hesitated for a brief moment, the weight of secrecy evident even across the digital line. "It's complicated. Just trust me on this. You need to get to a location outside the city. Send me your coordinates, and a team will meet you there."

Shade's gaze swept over the bustling crowd outside the cafe window, his mind already calculating possible exit routes. "And what's the code word? I don't plan on getting into anyone's car without it."

Marcus chuckled softly, a familiar sound that put Shade at ease. "Crows at Midnight."

Shade smirked. "Seriously? Bit dramatic, don't you think?"

"It'll do the job," Marcus replied. "Just be ready. And Shade—this is big. Don't take unnecessary risks."

Shade hung up, turning back to Cho, who was zipping up a worn-out duffel bag filled with their tech equipment. "We've got a ride coming. Time to move."

While Shade was busy making preparations, Marcus was pulling strings behind the scenes with Harrows, who was contacting some of his old military friends. These were men he'd served with during numerous campaigns, trusted allies who had seen the best and worst humanity had to offer. Harrows paced the wooden floor of Dr. Shaw's family house, phone pressed to his ear as he spoke in low, urgent tones. He asked if it were possible for the US military to assist in the discreet movement of equipment and personnel to a secret location. They were planning on operating in the shadows to ensure the required weaponry and mechanics could be created, tested, and arranged in the least time they had.

Harrows detailed the plan, explaining that the equipment from the bio unit facilities, including nanotech, needed to be relocated overseas. The chaos at New Dawn and the LHC's presence in the States made it crucial to separate these assets from the epicenter of unrest.

"We're moving them to an underground bunker facility in Ukraine," Harrows finished, aware of the audacity of his request. "It's NATO territory—a secure location for what we need."

Rick Prescott, the man on the other end, was silent for a moment before he agreed, recognizing the urgency. "Alright, Harrows. I'll inform Sam and make it happen. But remember, this stays off the books. Any blowback, and you're on your own."

"Understood," Harrows replied, relief flooding through him. "Thank you, Rick. This means a lot."

* * *

Cho slung the duffel bag over his shoulder, glancing at Shade as they walked out into the streets. "So, where are we headed?"

"Open highway," Shade replied cryptically, leading the way out of the residential area. The bustling streets of Manila stretched out before them, filled with people going about their day, blissfully unaware of the secret operations unfolding in their midst.

As they made their way through the crowded sidewalks, Shade couldn't shake the feeling of being watched—a lingering paranoia that came with the territory of his work. He pulled up the hood of his jacket, casting a shadow over his face, and instructed Cho to do the same. The coordinates led them to an industrial area on the outskirts of the city, where old warehouses lined the streets, their faded facades testament to a bygone era. It was the perfect place for a discreet extraction, away from prying eyes and curious onlookers.

Shade glanced around, assessing the environment. The area was quiet, save for the distant hum of machinery and the occasional bark of stray dogs. He felt a familiar thrill of anticipation, the kind that came with operating on the edge of the law. Cho shifted nervously beside him, casting furtive glances around the desolate street.

"You sure this is the place?" he asked, a note of uncertainty in his voice.

"It is," Shade confirmed, spotting the subtle marks Marcus had instructed him to look for—a pair of intersecting lines etched into the concrete wall, barely noticeable unless you knew where to look. A sleek black SUV approached from the far end of the street, its headlights cutting through the gloom. Shade tensed, watching as the vehicle slowed to a stop in front of them. The driver's side window rolled down, revealing a stern-faced man wearing aviator sunglasses; his expression was neutral.

"Crows at Midnight," the man intoned, his voice a low rumble that carried authority.

Shade allowed himself a brief smirk, recognizing the code word. He reached into his pocket and pulled out a mask, slipping it over his face. Trust was a luxury he couldn't afford, not even with Marcus' assurances.

"Let's go," Shade instructed Cho, gesturing for him to climb into the backseat.

As they settled into the SUV, the vehicle's engine roared to life, and they sped away from the warehouse district, leaving behind the uncertainty of Manila for the unknown awaiting them. Shade stared out the window, watching the cityscape blur into a tapestry of lights and shadows. He was aware of the enormity of the mission ahead and the role he would play in it. Whatever Marcus had planned, Shade knew it involved more than just them—what he didn't know was that key figures and technologies were being moved across continents, away from the volatile ground zero of the States.

The New Dawn Facility was in utter shock and shambles ever since that broadcast in the morning. Many of the staff members had resorted to immediate resignation, while others had simply begun to speculate and argue. Dr. Shaw had recently been informed by Marcus that Harrows was conducting a covert shift of operation houses. She had passed the information to the few trustable subordinates left, one of which included Jeremiah Smith. He, upon learning of this, had arranged for a team of technicians to explain the situation to them and ask if they would volunteer for the task. Out of the initial eighteen, only five, including Thomas, had decided to take on the risky journey for the sake of their country (and perhaps a chance to be a part of something like *Secret Invasion,* as Thomas had claimed).

Dr. Shaw approached Nadia with the heavy subject. She was not sure how to ask a young woman with a family and a blooming social life to abandon it for God knows how long in an icy bunker off the coast of Europe. To her surprise and gratitude, she agreed almost immediately, though, on the condition that Dr. Shaw would keep her parents from knowing the truth as she did not wish to worry them.

It was endearing, really. The technicians, physicists, biologists, etc, fresh-faced and even veterans, each had their own little bubbles of happiness that seemed so insignificant against the big picture, yet it was those little things that kept their humanity alive. It strengthened their spirits and gave them the motivation to assist in any way they could.

Nevertheless, in a matter of a few hours, Unit 07 of the bio-chemical labs and nano technologies were cleared out by soldiers in civilian clothing that made them blend in with the usual employees of the facility. Dr. Shaw exchanged a look with Jeremiah, who looked like he was going to be sick.

"I hope your friends know what they're doing, Eve," he said, sighing as he rubbed the upper part of his stomach.

"I don't think they do, Jeremy, but they're trying. We all have to…The LHC needs to be dismantled." Her eyes remained on the floor as she leaned against his side. "No matter what Anya says anymore."

"Parker is on it. He's got the boys and Debbie taking it apart as we speak. We removed the generator, so it shouldn't be a problem."

* * *

It was evening in Switzerland, where the Cabal's physical meeting was being held. Dr. Anton Weiss sat opposite Helena Voss as another distinguished member explained the current global situation.

"How are our friends in the East doing?" Helena's voice was velvety as she inclined her head, her silvery-blond hair shimmering in the candlelight.

"The media corporations there trying to get as many spokespeople on it to make sure the demonstrations cannot be swept under the rug." The response was measured and simple. "Although the more orthodox counties have shown resilience, there is no doubt that many would come around to the idea of the new dawn."

A tall, elegant man seated at the far end voiced his query. "And when do we get to see them? The beings from beyond the veil?"

Murmurs of agreement to his question rose from the table.

This time, it was Dr. Weiss who gave the answer. "Tomorrow night. Under the full moon, since the energy source works better with a specific gravitational setting. One which can only be accomplished under a full moon's night under a clear sky. Hence, why," he paused to gesture vaguely around the room, "we are here, in this country, near the mountains, to ensure the portal can be accessed without the risk of a failure."

"I thought the source was in the States?" Helena inquired once Weiss sat down.

"The one there is a minor piece to keep the generator running. The real nuclear source is right here, along with a better, more stable copy of the LHC. I had taken the liberty of making sure this was being built at the same time as the one for *Exodia*." Weiss' voice was collected, but there was an excited edge to it as well. One which mirrored Voss' own anticipation for a world where they could be overlords.

Not just humans with material sources at their disposal but beings with absolute power.

* * *

Highway M06, near Lviv, Ukraine

04 30

The early morning air was crisp and carried a biting chill, the Ukrainian sky a deep navy, pierced by the first light of dawn. The vast, deserted stretch of Highway M06 near Lviv was still and silent, save for the low rumble of a sleek US stealth plane touching down smoothly onto the makeshift airstrip. The plane glided to a halt, its engines hissing softly in the predawn silence. It was a marvel of modern engineering, designed for speed and stealth, its matte black surface absorbing the dim light. This was a covert operation, kept under the radar to ensure that the critical mission went unnoticed by prying eyes.

A mile or so from the highway stood the entrance to an underground bunker hidden amongst the natural topography of the land. It was a relic from the Cold War, repurposed now for a new kind of battle—a battle against the unknown entities and technologies that threatened the very fabric of reality. Around the perimeter, military guards patrolled in stealthy formations, their movements synchronized and precise, ensuring that the area was secure from any potential threats.

The stealth plane's cargo doors opened with a hydraulic hiss, revealing a team of soldiers who quickly began unloading crates of equipment, containers holding the latest nanotechnology, and even the heavily secured pod that contained the recaptured entity—a creature of immense power and unknown origins that had recently escaped the confines of its previous facility. Automated assistance drones hovered nearby, waiting to aid in the meticulous setup of the new laboratory space meters underground.

Shade squinted against the dim light as he was roughly guided out of the plane. The cool air hit him like a wave, and he took a deep breath, trying to shake off the remnants of sleep deprivation. As he stumbled onto the tarmac, he noticed the bustling activity around him. Soldiers moved with purpose, their faces set in stoic determination as they managed the logistics of the operation. He felt a shove from behind urging him forward, and he complied, albeit begrudgingly. His eyes swept over the scene, taking in every detail. They were a mile from the entrance to the underground bunker, its concealed hatch barely visible in the dim light of the early morning. The place was buzzing with cold efficiency, a show of the military precision that orchestrated such covert endeavors.

The convoy of military vehicles lined up on the side of the highway hummed quietly, waiting for the next phase of their mission. One of the vehicles caught Shade's attention—a transport truck marked with US military emblem. Its doors opened, and a soldier, clad in a tactical uniform and bearing the rigid posture typical of his kind, stepped forward.

Shade's eyes narrowed as he watched the soldier approach the vehicle's rear door, his movements surprisingly gentle for someone of his stature. He opened the door, extending a hand to coax whoever was inside to step out.

From the shadowed interior of the truck emerged a young woman, her presence immediately recognizable to Shade. She was Marcus' niece, Nadia Ayoub. Her long dark hair was slightly tousled, a stark contrast to the crispness of her surroundings. She appeared slightly disoriented, her eyes adjusting to the pale light as she was steadied by the soldier.

Of course, she gets special treatment, Shade thought, arching an eyebrow.

Behind her, a gangly young man with a head of ridiculous, unkempt hair climbed out, looking slightly bewildered. His attire, slightly disheveled from the journey, marked him as someone unaccustomed to such military environments. This was Thomas Anderson, the technician from the facility, Shade surmised. Shade watched them with an expression caught between amusement and mild irritation. They didn't seem to notice him or the other operatives around them; their focus was directed entirely toward the imposing soldier leading them toward the entrance of the underground bunker.

As they walked, Nadia clutched a small satchel close to her side, her mind overflowing with thoughts about the new assignment and the responsibilities it entailed. Thomas walked slightly behind her, casting nervous glances at the military personnel, his eyes wide with a mixture of awe and unease. The soldier leading them stopped at a heavily secured hatch embedded into the ground. With a series of coded inputs and biometric scans, the hatch released its locks with a low rumble, revealing a staircase that descended into the earth. The bunker lay below, a complex of sterile corridors and cutting-edge laboratories designed for one purpose: to contain and study the very elements that had prompted this underground mission.

Shade found himself momentarily captivated by the sight of Nadia and Thomas disappearing into the depths of the bunker. He wondered what they knew about the true nature of their task here—how much Marcus had disclosed to his niece about the gravity of the situation they were entangled in. A soldier shoved Shade again, snapping him out of his reverie.

"Get moving," the soldier barked, gesturing for him to follow the path that Nadia and Thomas had taken.

The descent into the bunker was steep and disorienting, the stairway lit by dim overhead lights that cast long shadows on the metallic walls. As Shade reached the bottom, he found himself in a sprawling underground facility, the scale of which was far greater than he had anticipated. The air was cool and sterile, the faint hum of ventilation systems echoing through the expansive corridors.

He followed the trail of soldiers and equipment, passing by labs already bustling with activity. Scientists and technicians were busy setting up workstations, unpacking crates of equipment, and calibrating instruments. The atmosphere was a blend of urgency and meticulous precision.

Shade finally caught up with Nadia and Thomas in a large central chamber that served as the facility's nerve center. The room was dominated by a massive digital display, showing real-time data feeds and security footage from various points across the compound. It was here that the core team would coordinate their efforts to study and contain the entities and technologies brought over from the States. Nadia stood by one of the consoles, already engrossed in her work. Thomas was nearby, adjusting settings on a bank of computers, his initial nervousness giving way to a focused intensity.

As the initial briefing concluded, Shade made his way to his assigned quarters—a small, sparsely furnished room equipped with the essentials. It was a stark contrast to the bustling activity outside, offering a brief respite from the stress of the mission. He sat on the edge of the bed, processing the events that had brought him here. The stakes were high, and the path ahead was littered with uncertainty, but Shade thrived in such conditions. It was the thrill of the unknown that drove him forward.

And just like that. It was decided.

The Military bunker was to be used as a secret base for experimentation and study of captured entities, along with the creation of weaponry to fend off those specific creatures. Meanwhile, the New Dawn facility will continue to operate as intended, with the esteemed Dr. Evelyn Shaw and her small band of rebels playing double agents to Dr. Weiss' nefarious plans.

The situation of the world outside the walls of either facility was dire, and should the worst befall them, it was anyone's guess how bloody things could get. Thus was the nature of the arrival of a new dawn.

Chapter 6: Fractures

The skies of a remote fjords of Norway had been calm and clear just moments before, offering a stunning contrast to the violent events that were about to unfold. The first sign of the impending catastrophe was a strange, iridescent shimmer that appeared in the sky, growing larger and more vivid with each passing second. It was as if the very fabric of reality was being stretched, thinning to the point where another world was beginning to bleed through.

The shimmer warped into a swirling vortex, a tear in the sky that crackled with unnatural energy. From the center of the portal, a dark void spread, devouring the blue sky. The wind picked up, howling with an eerie, otherworldly sound as the tear widened. The portal, now a gaping wound in the heavens, revealed glimpses of something incomprehensible on the other side—a writhing mass of shapes and colors that defied logic and reason.

As the portal stabilized, things began to emerge. Shadows, at first, indistinct and shifting, but soon they took on forms—twisted, elongated figures that moved with an unnatural fluidity. They were eldritch creatures, neither fully corporeal nor entirely ethereal, their bodies a disturbing blend of tendrils, eyes, and mouths that gaped in silent screams. They descended upon the fjords, their presence warping the landscape around them. The waters of the fjord turned black, churning with malevolent energy as the creatures began to spread across the land, bringing with them an aura of despair and madness.

But the disarray was not limited to air, for deep beneath the icy waters of the Barents Sea, near the continental shelf, another dimensional tear was wreaking havoc on the natural world. The portal here was less visible but no less destructive. It was a faint glow, hidden from the surface by the crushing depths of the ocean. This tear pulsed with a sickly green light, radiating energy that seeped into the surrounding waters, altering everything it touched.

At first, the changes were subtle. Fish and other marine life began to act erratically, swimming in tight circles or darting aimlessly through the water. But soon, the mutations began. Creatures of the deep were twisted into monstrous forms by the corrupting influence of the portal. A school of fish fused together into a writhing, multi-headed abomination, their scales glowing with unnatural bioluminescence. A giant squid, its body distorted by the energy, grew to an impossible size, its tentacles elongating and branching into tendrils that seemed to have a mind of their own, seeking out and ensnaring anything that came too close.

The sea floor itself began to change. Coral reefs that had stood for millennia started to twist and mutate, growing into towering, spiked structures that pulsed with the same green light as the portal. The very water around the tear became thick and viscous, more like oil than seawater, and it began to spread, slowly corrupting the ocean far beyond the initial tear.

Meanwhile, unbeknownst to the world, in the heart of Iceland, where the dormant volcano Eyjafjallajökull lay quiet under a thick layer of ice and ash, a different kind of doom was stirring. Deep within the bowels of the earth, beneath the volcanic rock, another portal had torn through the fabric of reality. This one glowed with a deep, molten red, casting an ominous light through the magma chambers of the volcano.

The tear was not content to merely sit beneath the earth; it called to something ancient, something that had slumbered for eons beneath the volcano. The ground began to shake, a low rumble that grew in intensity until the very mountain seemed to be alive with anger. The magma, once sluggish and cool, began to churn violently, glowing brighter as it was infused with the energy of the tear.

Then, from within the molten depths, *it* began to rise.

The entity was enormous, a titan of unimaginable size, its form barely distinguishable from the molten rock that surrounded it. It was as if the volcano itself had come to life but twisted into something far more sinister. The creature's body was a mass of seething lava and hardened rock, its limbs elongated and jagged. It had no face, only a massive, gaping maw that stretched across what could only be described as its head, spewing fire and ash with every movement.

As it rose, the volcano erupted with a force that shook the entire island, sending rivers of lava cascading down its sides. The sky above darkened as ash and smoke filled the air, blotting out the sun. The titan, now fully emerged from its fiery prison, stood taller than any mountain, its presence a cataclysmic force of destruction.

The earth quaked beneath its massive feet as it began to move, each step sending shockwaves through the ground. The once-dormant volcano had become a living nightmare, its fiery breath scorching the land as it began its march of annihilation, leaving nothing but molten rock and ash in its wake.

* * *

The early morning sun barely pierced the thick layer of clouds hanging over Fort Blackwood, a sprawling military base nestled deep within the rugged terrain of the Rocky Mountains. The base was alive with the hum of activity, soldiers marching in formation, and the distant roar of jet engines preparing for take-off. However, the real action was taking place within one of the heavily guarded hangars on the eastern edge of the base.

Inside the hangar, a different kind of chaos unfolded. Engineers and technicians bustled around, making last-minute adjustments to a variety of experimental equipment—sleek, black-armored suits that looked more like something out of a sci-fi movie than a standard military issue. On one side of the hangar, a line of soldiers stood at attention, each waiting to be fitted with the advanced nano-tech gear that had been covertly transferred from the New Dawn facility.

At the center of this operation stood Major General Samuel Whitmore, a man in his early fifties with a stern expression that rarely softened. His uniform was pristine, adorned with medals and insignias that spoke of a lifetime of service. Beside him, John Harrows, a tall, imposing figure with a military bearing, discussed the final preparations. Harrows' voice was low, but there was an edge to it, a sense of urgency that matched the grimness of the situation.

"We've successfully integrated the nano-tech into the armor and weapons systems, but there's still fine-tuning to be done," Harrows said, his gaze shifting to the soldiers who were now being fitted with the gear. "They need to be ready for whatever comes through that portal. We can't afford any mistakes."

Whitmore nodded, his eyes narrowing slightly as he observed the men suiting up. "We've come too far to falter now. This crusade we've embarked on—it's the only way to protect our world. The cabal, those beings from the other side—they won't stop until they've overrun everything. The tech from New Dawn will give us the edge we need."

On the other side of the hangar, Marcus Flynn leaned against a metal pillar, the tip of his cigarette glowing faintly. His eyes, tired yet vigilant, watched the proceedings with a mixture of unease and resignation. The past few weeks had been a whirlwind of revelations and close calls, and now, standing in this hangar filled with cutting-edge military tech, the reality of the situation weighed heavily on him.

A few soldiers glanced his way, curious about the civilian who was in their midst, but Marcus paid them no mind. His thoughts were elsewhere, particularly on the cryptic warning he'd received from Shade. The beings they were dealing with were unlike anything humanity had encountered before—entities that could be elemental in nature. The memory of Shade's voice on the other end of the line still echoed in his mind.

Marcus took another drag from his cigarette, exhaling slowly as he watched a group of soldiers being fitted with the tech gear. "You know," he said, his voice carrying just enough to reach Harrows, "these things could be elemental, according to a source of mine. One of them was electricity-based, or at least something close to it. Not saying it's gospel, but it's worth keeping in mind."

Harrows glanced over at Marcus, his expression unreadable. He didn't ask who the source was—he knew better than to pry into Flynn's connections. "We've considered that possibility," Harrows replied evenly. "In fact, it might explain some of the anomalies we've been seeing. The entity we captured, the one we've sent to the underground bunker in Ukraine, has been showing signs of energy manipulation. That's why we brought in Thomas Anderson and your niece, Nadia. They've been making progress, but it's slow-going."

Marcus nodded, flicking the ash from his cigarette. The mention of Nadia stirred a protective instinct in him, but he pushed it down. He trusted her abilities—she was brilliant, after all—but the danger she was in weighed heavily on his conscience. "I hope they're prepared for what they might be dealing with over there," he muttered, more to himself than anyone else.

Whitmore, catching the tail end of Marcus' words, turned to Harrows. "The personnel we've sent to Ukraine are some of the best we have, both military and civilian. If anyone can crack this, it's them. But we need to stay focused here. If these entities are truly elemental, we need to be ready for anything."

Harrows nodded in agreement, his gaze hardening. "We will be. And when the time comes, we'll be ready to take the fight to them."

As the final preparations continued, the atmosphere in the hangar grew tense, collective anticipation hanging in the air. Fort Blackwood, once a regular military base, was now the frontline in a battle that few outside its walls could even comprehend. The soldiers being fitted with the advanced tech had no idea what they would soon be facing, but they were ready—ready to fight and, if necessary, ready to die for a cause they barely understood.

And as Marcus Flynn watched the soldiers, he couldn't help but wonder just how prepared they all truly were for the horrors that awaited them beyond the veil.

* * *

The air inside the underground chamber was thick with tension, a profound mix of anxiety and grim determination. Fluorescent lights cast an eerie glow over the scene, highlighting the maze of cables and machinery that made up the heart of the Large Hadron Collider (LHC). Technicians and engineers—referred to by Jeremiah Smith as "The Boys and Debbie"—moved with precision and caution, their movements deliberate as they prepared to dismantle the generator. Each person was clad in protective clothing and hazmat suits, the thick material shielding them from the potentially catastrophic effects of the nuclear reactive energy source they were about to extract.

The generator itself was a behemoth of technology, a tangled web of wires and metallic surfaces that hummed with a low, almost imperceptible vibration. The air around it seemed to crackle with the latent power contained within. Jeremiah, overseeing the operation from a nearby console, barked out orders, his voice carrying a mixture of authority and urgency. The subordinates responded with quick nods, their faces hidden behind the reflective visors of their suits.

One of the engineers carefully inserted a specialized tool into a slot in the generator, causing a panel to hiss open, revealing the glowing core within. The core pulsed with an unnatural light, a sickly green that cast long shadows on the walls. The team held their breath as they began the delicate task of extracting the energy source, each movement slow and calculated.

Meanwhile, outside the containment area, Dr. Evelyn Shaw stood near the entrance, her gloved hands gripping a tablet as she reviewed the latest updates. The air in the corridor was cool, a stark contrast to the oppressive atmosphere inside. Her brow furrowed as she listened intently to Marcus Flynn, who was on the other end of a secure communication line.

"Shade's going to manage the network lines from the bunker in Ukraine," Marcus said, his voice steady despite the gravity of the situation. "He'll make sure our communications are protected from any adversaries. We can't afford any leaks, not with what's at stake."

Dr. Shaw nodded, though Marcus couldn't see her. "Good. We need every advantage we can get." She paused, glancing back at the sealed door behind her, where the extraction was taking place. "Nadia's been working tirelessly. She reported encapsulating four other entities over the past seven hours. Each one… more grotesque than the last."

Marcus exhaled sharply on the other end of the line, and Dr. Shaw could almost picture him taking a drag from his ever-present cigarette.

"Tell me about them," he said, his voice a mix of curiosity and dread.

Dr. Shaw hesitated; the horrors Nadia had described were still fresh in her mind. "The first entity—well, it's not even a single organism. It's symbiotic, a collective of parasitic beings that infest a host and slowly consume them from the inside out. The scavenging soldiers who first encountered it didn't stand a chance. By the time they realized what they were dealing with, entire units were gone, absorbed into this… thing. Nadia said the host bodies look like they're alive, but only just. They're hollowed out, mere shells."

Marcus remained silent, allowing her to continue.

"The second one… it's an aberration, even by the standards we've come to expect. Its body is covered in eyes—dozens, maybe hundreds of them. They're not just for seeing, though. They're parasitic. Any living creature it touches begins to sprout eyes as well, inside and out. It starts with the skin; then, the eyes begin to grow inward, covering the organs and blocking airways. The victims suffocate, or worse. The scientists have retrieved a few of the victims—animals, humans, and a few unfortunate soldiers. The autopsies… were nauseating."

At that, he let out a low whistle. "That's… something."

"And that's just the beginning," Dr. Shaw continued, her voice tight. "The third entity is a mass of tendrils, each one tipped with a sharp, bone-like claw. It moves like liquid, but those tendrils can harden in an instant, slicing through anything in its path. She reported that the soldiers had to resort to flamethrowers to keep it at bay, but even then, it was more a deterrent than a solution."

"What about the fourth?" Marcus asked, his voice a little quieter now.

"The fourth one is… amorphous. It doesn't have a fixed shape. One minute, it's a mist; the next, it's a solid mass. It seems to adapt to its surroundings, but its most terrifying aspect is its ability to replicate. It splits, creating identical copies of itself. Each copy is just as dangerous as the original. The scientists think it's some kind of survival mechanism, but they haven't been able to study it for long— every time they think they've contained it, it finds a way to break free."

Marcus let out a slow breath. "And the lass handling all this?"

"She's doing more than handling it," Dr. Shaw said, her voice softening slightly with pride. "She's found weaknesses in each of them, ways to counter their abilities. She's already sent the reports to the base in the Rocky Mountains. Shade's been overseeing the transmissions." A small smile formed on her lips as she, perhaps hoping to lighten the mood ever so slightly, added another detail, "She called him 'creepy eyes'—said he looks at her as if he were a snake."

"Sounds like her," Marcus replied, a hint of a smile in his voice despite the grim subject matter. "I'll pass the word along. Let's just hope the tech can keep up with whatever's coming next."

As the conversation ended, Dr. Shaw took a moment to steady herself. The enormity of what they were dealing with was almost too much to comprehend. But there was no time for hesitation, no room for doubt. The world was on the brink, and it was up to them—scientists, soldiers, journalists, and yes, even cyber terrorists—to pull it back from the edge.

She turned back to the sealed door, where Jeremiah and the team were nearing the final stages of the extraction. Whatever was happening at the LHC, whatever forces had been unleashed, they had to contain it. The future of humanity depended on it.

The sound of the extraction process hummed behind the heavy doors, but her mind was elsewhere, lost in memories that she had buried deep.

Evelyn had always been curious about the universe. As a child, she would lie on the roof of her home, staring up at the stars, asking her mother endless questions about the cosmos. Her mother, an astrophysicist with a mind as vast as the universe she studied, had always encouraged her. It was her mother's passion that had ignited Evelyn's own, driving her to pursue physics with an intensity that left little room for anything else.

Her journey had been relentless—excelling in her studies, earning her PhD in particle physics from MIT, and eventually finding herself at the forefront of ground-breaking research. The LHC was supposed to be the pinnacle of her career, the culmination of years of hard work and dedication. But it had also brought with it the kind of ethical dilemmas that she had never fully prepared for. The dimensional breach had been the tipping point, a moment when the pursuit of knowledge collided with the terrifying reality of what that knowledge could unleash.

But it wasn't just the science that weighed on her. There was a personal connection, a shadow that loomed over her every step—the mysterious disappearance of her mother. For years, it had been an unsolved mystery, a painful wound that never fully healed. But around a decade ago, through Dr. Weiss' documentation, she had stumbled upon information that suggested her mother's disappearance might be tied to early, secret experiments related to earlier prototypes of the LHC. The thought that her work might be connected to her mother's fate was both haunting and motivating, driving her to push forward, even when doubt and fear threatened to paralyze her.

Her thoughts drifted to Jeremiah, the veteran engineer who had been by her side through so many trials. He had been more than just a colleague; he had been a constant presence, a stabilizing force in the chaotic world of high-stakes science. There had been a time, two or three years ago when they had worked so closely that their connection had started to transcend the professional.

The LHC for *Exodia* had still been under construction then, and the project had been fraught with challenges—some of which had turned deadly. Jeremiah was her rock during those times, quietly supporting her even as the pressure mounted. But Evelyn, consumed by the pursuit of progress, had distanced herself from him. She had insisted on pushing forward, even in the face of mounting casualties, dismissing the dangers as the inevitable costs of progress. Jeremiah had never blamed her, at least not out loud, but she knew that her refusal to take responsibility for the accidents had created a rift between them.

She had pushed him away, just as she had pushed away anyone who threatened to get too close. The potential for love had been there, something real and tangible, but it had never been allowed to blossom. Instead, it had withered on the vine, leaving behind a formality that now defined their relationship. They were still civil and still worked well together, but the easy camaraderie they had once shared was gone, replaced by a distance that she could feel every time they were in the same room.

As she stood there, reflecting on all that had been lost—both personally and professionally—Evelyn felt a warmth rise in her chest. It was a familiar feeling, one that she had often pushed aside but could never fully ignore. It was the warmth of Jeremiah's presence, the memory of what they had once been and what they could have been if she had only allowed it. The thought brought a flush to her cheeks, an involuntary reaction that she quickly tried to suppress.

With a heavy sigh, Evelyn forced herself to focus back on the present. There was no time for regrets, not now. The world was teetering on the edge of an abyss, and she had a job to do. Whatever her personal feelings, whatever her fears and doubts, they would have to wait. There was too much at stake.

* * *

The atmosphere in the underground bunker was tense, the air thick with a mix of anticipation and anxiety. Nadia Ayoub stood before the control panel, her eyes fixed on the bulletproof chamber where the first captured entity was being observed. The creature, with its elongated limbs and snout, moved with an unsettling grace, its alien form both fascinating and terrifying.

Nadia had insisted on releasing the creature, whom she had taken the liberty to name Casca, into the chamber, confident that "he" merely needed to stretch his limbs and acclimate to his new environment. For a while, everything seemed to be going smoothly. The creature ambled around the enclosure, dipping its head to sniff at the ground before devouring the raw meat provided. It ate like a dog, ravenously tearing into the flesh, its teeth gnashing with a ferocity that sent chills down the spines of the observing scientists.

Nadia watched closely, her fingers hovering over the control panel. The creature's behavior was almost... docile. It moved with a strange kind of curiosity, exploring the enclosure, its snout twitching as it took in the unfamiliar scents. Nadia felt a small surge of relief. Perhaps, as she had hoped, the creature could be studied without incident. She was just about to begin testing its memory retention when the creature's demeanor changed in an instant. It was starting to become obvious that this particular one was not being studied just for her to find a weakness.

Without warning, the creature bolted across the enclosure, slamming its elongated body into the glass with a force that rattled the chamber. The sound reverberated through the room, a loud, jarring echo that made several scientists jump back in alarm. Nadia's heart raced as she saw the creature recoil and then charge again, this time with even more force. It wasn't merely testing its environment—it was attacking it.

Several scientists instinctively banged on the glass, hoping the noise would startle the creature, but their actions only seemed to agitate it further. The creature's elongated limbs pounded against the glass, its snout scraping along the surface as it tried to force its way through. Nadia could see the fury in its eyes, a wild, untamed rage that made her stomach churn. The creature wasn't just an animal— it was something far more dangerous, something that could not be contained by mere glass and steel.

Realizing the situation was spiraling out of control, Nadia quickly activated the control panel, releasing a dense cloud of gas into the enclosure. The gas was designed to subdue the creature, to calm its frantic movements, but as the fog filled the chamber, Nadia could only hope it would work in time. The creature continued to thrash, its body slamming against the glass with a sickening thud, each impact causing the entire room to shudder.

Meanwhile, in the comms room, Thomas Anderson was sweating bullets as he relayed information to John Harrows at the fort in the Rocky Mountains. The comms were patched through to a large monitor, the connection stable but the tension palpable. Thomas' voice trembled slightly as he explained the various items used to fend off the newly captured entities.

"We've been working on specialized containment and countermeasures," Thomas explained, his voice carrying through the speaker. "The first entity, the one you're observing now, responds negatively to intense light and certain ultrasonic frequencies. We've integrated those into the enclosures to keep them under control."

His voice wavered as he moved on to the more gruesome details. "For the second entity... we call it *Scourge*, the one that feeds on organic matter by rapidly decomposing it—extremely acidic—it's been encapsulated in a reinforced container lined with a neutralizing agent. Even then, the containment needs to be replaced regularly because the entity slowly corrodes the materials over time. We have managed to create long-range firearms that are laced with the same agent; they would dissolve within the body when hit, so, uh, that should help against those."

Thomas took a deep breath, his eyes darting nervously as he continued. "The third entity is... more challenging. It's... symbiotic. We've observed that it can merge with other organisms, taking over their nervous system and enhancing their physical capabilities. This one has been encapsulated in a liquid medium that slows down its metabolic processes, but it's a temporary measure at best."

The room was dead silent as Thomas paused before addressing the last and most horrific of the entities. "The fourth one... we've started calling it *Pink Eye*. It's covered in parasitic eyes that sprout on any living being it touches. The eyes spread rapidly, overtaking orifices and growing inside the body until the host is completely consumed. The current containment protocol involves keeping it in a vacuum-sealed chamber where it's deprived of any biological material to infect. However, the eyes... they still seem to 'watch' us through the glass."

As he mentioned Pink Eye, there was a collective shiver in the room. Even the seasoned army technicians and artillery experts seemed unnerved by the description, their faces pale as they absorbed the information. They quickly began preparing blueprints, discussing ways to integrate the defensive measures into their weapons and armor. But the unsettling knowledge that these creatures could not only escape but could also pose an unprecedented threat to humanity hung over them like a dark cloud.

Major General Whitmore, who had been observing the scene with an intense scowl, barked at Thomas to move things along faster. "We don't have time for hesitation, Anderson! I want those prototypes ready and tested before we're dealing with these things on the battlefield!"

Thomas stuttered, his hands trembling slightly as he tried to assure the general. "W-we're also sending the first prototypes for the extended armor to fight off Pink Eye's kind. They'll have integrated sensors to detect the spread of the parasitic eyes, and the armor itself will be coated with a substance that... that... uh, repels the growth. But we're still in the early stages of testing..."

Whitmore's glare could have cut through steel. "Early stages won't cut it, son. Get it done, or we'll be the ones with those damned eyes sprouting out of our skulls!"

The general's harsh words echoed in the room, the gravity of the situation sinking in for everyone present. Thomas swallowed hard, nodding furiously as he tried to regain his composure. The world was currently being invaded by something incomprehensible, and failure was not an option. As the call ended, the comms room was left in a heavy silence, the weight of their mission bearing down on them with an almost tangible force.

Back in the observation chamber, Nadia watched as the gas finally began to take effect, the creature's thrashing slowing down until it collapsed in a heap on the floor, its elongated limbs sprawled out awkwardly. The immediate danger had passed, but Nadia knew that this was only the beginning. The creatures they had captured were unlike anything they had ever encountered before, and the challenges ahead were as terrifying as they were unknown.

Her heart pounded as she made the decision to override the protests of the other doctors and soldiers. The room buzzed with tense energy as she reached for the control panel, her fingers hesitating for only a moment before undoing the locks to the chamber. The bulletproof door hissed open, and she stepped inside, the heavy steel groaning as it sealed shut behind her.

The creature, which was now slumped on the floor in a hazy, half-asleep state, was a pitiful sight. Its elongated limbs twitched occasionally, the snout resting on the cold floor, nostrils flaring gently as it breathed in the gas that still lingered in the chamber. The lavender and citrusy scent that wafted through the room was unexpected, a stark contrast to the pungent, acrid odors usually associated with such situations.

She knelt beside the creature, her hand trembling slightly as she gently tugged at its limb, coaxing it to a more comfortable position. The creature responded sluggishly, its mouth twitching and jerking as if unable to control its movements. To her, it seemed almost... vulnerable. A part of her felt a strange fascination with this specific being, a sense of responsibility for its well-being, even in captivity.

But the others in the room didn't share her sentiments.

"What the hell is she doing?" one of the scientists, Dr. Reynolds, muttered angrily under his breath. His face was flushed with anger as he watched Nadia's actions through the thick glass. "That thing should be sedated, not lulled to sleep with some... some aromatherapy bullshit!"

Another scientist, Dr. Carter, nodded in agreement, his expression just as livid. "She's coddling it like it's a dog! This isn't a pet, it's a damn alien entity! It's dangerous, and she's putting all of us at risk with her reckless behavior!"

Reynolds' scowl deepened as he turned to one of the nearby soldiers. "Get me a line to Dr. Shaw. She needs to know about this. She is too soft for this work. She's going to cause serious damage with her... her carelessness."

As the soldier hurried to comply, Reynolds and Carter exchanged a look of mutual frustration, their anger simmering just below the surface. Nadia's unorthodox methods were seen as a threat to the entire operation and they were determined to see her removed from the project.

* * *

Boston, Massachusetts, USA
Wednesday 05:43 PM

The streets of Boston had become a war zone. The once bustling city was now a crumbling battleground, littered with debris and the bodies of those who had fallen in the fight against the emerging horrors. Smoke billowed from the ruins of skyscrapers, and the constant sound of gunfire echoed through the air, mingled with the shrieks of terror and the inhuman roars of the invaders.

In the heart of the city, a group of Marines, led by Sergeant Jackson, was engaged in a brutal firefight against a horde of eldritch creatures that had emerged from a dimensional breach in the harbor. These beings were unlike anything they had ever seen—massive, writhing forms of tangled limbs and pulsating flesh, their bodies adorned with eyes that glowed a sickly green. They moved with a terrifying grace, slithering and lurching forward, tearing through buildings and vehicles as if they were made of paper.

"Hold the line!" Sergeant Jackson shouted over the roar of gunfire, his voice barely audible above the chaos. "We can't let them push us back any further!"

The Marines fought valiantly, their weapons blazing as they unleashed round after round into the advancing creatures. But for every one they took down, another seemed to take its place. The ground beneath their feet was slick with blood and ichor, and the air was thick with the stench of death.

One of the creatures, larger than the others, lunged at Jackson, its maw wide open, revealing rows of jagged, needle-like teeth. Jackson barely had time to react, firing his weapon into the creature's gaping mouth. The bullets tore through its flesh, but it barely slowed, its momentum carrying it forward as it slammed into Jackson, sending him crashing to the ground.

The creature loomed over him, its many eyes locking onto his, and for a brief moment, Jackson felt a deep, primal fear grip him. But he refused to give in. With a grunt of effort, he rolled to the side, grabbing a nearby grenade and pulling the pin. As the creature lunged again, Jackson jammed the grenade into its mouth and rolled away.

The explosion was deafening, and the creature's head was blown apart in a shower of gore. Jackson scrambled to his feet, bloodied but alive, and continued fighting. But as he looked around at the carnage, he knew that their chances of survival were slim. The creatures were relentless, and their numbers seemed endless.

As the battle raged on, Jackson couldn't help but think of the civilians who had been unable to escape the city. He had seen the remains of families torn apart, children's bodies cradled in their parents' arms as they tried to shield them from the horrors. It was a nightmare, one that he feared they wouldn't wake up from.

Buenos Aires, Argentina

Wednesday 06:43 PM

In the city of Buenos Aires, the people had fought back with a determination born of desperation. The beings that emerged from the breach here were strange, almost human-like in form, but twisted in ways that defied explanation. They had elongated limbs, their skin a mottled gray-green, and their faces were grotesque parodies of human features—eyes too large, mouths that stretched far too wide, and fingers that ended in razor-sharp claws.

The military had responded swiftly, setting up barricades and establishing zones of control, but the creatures were fast and cunning. They moved through the city in packs, hunting the living with a terrifying efficiency.

In one neighborhood, a group of residents had taken matters into their own hands. Armed with whatever they could find—kitchen knives, makeshift spears, and even Molotov cocktails—they had fortified a small apartment building, determined to protect their families and their homes.

Raúl, a former mechanic, led the group. His hands, once skilled in repairing engines, were now calloused and bloody from the constant fighting. He had seen too many of his neighbors fall, their bodies torn apart by the creatures, and he was determined not to let that happen again.

As night fell, the creatures came, their inhuman cries echoing through the streets. Raúl and his group fought bravely, hurling firebombs from the windows and stabbing at the creatures with makeshift weapons. The air was thick with smoke and the acrid smell of burning flesh, but they held their ground.

One of the creatures, larger and more ferocious than the others, broke through the barricade, its claws slashing through the air as it charged at Raúl. He met it head-on, driving his spear into its chest with all his strength. The creature shrieked in pain, but it didn't fall. Instead, it grabbed Raúl with its long, sinewy arms, lifting him off the ground as it opened its maw wide, preparing to devour him.

But Raúl didn't falter. With a final, desperate effort, he yanked a grenade from his belt and shoved it into the creature's mouth. As it bit down, the grenade exploded, and both Raúl and the creature were engulfed in flames.

The others watched in horror as their leader was consumed by fire, but his sacrifice bought them precious time. They redoubled their efforts, fighting with a ferocity that matched the creatures'. By dawn, the creatures were dead, and the apartment building still stood, but the cost had been high. Raúl and many others had given their lives, and the survivors knew that the fight was far from over.

Moscow, Russia

Wednesday 07:43 PM

Moscow was knee-deep in chaos. The sky above the city had taken on a strange, otherworldly hue, and the air was charged with a strange energy that made the hair on the back of one's neck stand on end. The creatures that had emerged from the breach here were entirely unlike anything seen before—large, insectoid beings with chitinous exoskeletons and multifaceted eyes that glowed with an eerie, unnatural light.

They moved in swarms, overwhelming the city's defenses with sheer numbers. The Russian military, known for its discipline and efficiency, had been caught off guard by the speed and ferocity of the attack. Tanks and armored vehicles rumbled through the streets, their cannons firing into the mass of creatures, but it was like trying to stop a tidal wave with a bucket.

Captain Ivanov was leading a unit of soldiers through the ruined streets, their mission to rescue a group of civilians trapped in a collapsed building. The creatures swarmed around them, their mandibles clicking and their wings buzzing as they closed in.

"Keep moving!" Ivanov shouted, his voice hoarse from barking orders. "We have to reach those people!"

The soldiers pressed on, firing at the creatures as they advanced. The air was filled with the sound of gunfire and the screeching of the insectoid beings as they fell under the relentless barrage. But for every creature they killed, more seemed to take its place.

As they reached the building, Ivanov spotted the civilians—an elderly couple, a young woman, and her child—huddled together in fear. He waved them over, urging them to move quickly, but as they started towards him, one of the creatures swooped down, its mandibles snapping shut around the young woman's leg.

She screamed in pain, collapsing to the ground as the creature began to drag her away. Ivanov didn't hesitate. He charged forward, slamming the butt of his rifle into the creature's head, trying to dislodge it. The creature let out a high-pitched screech, releasing the woman and turning its attention to Ivanov.

It lunged at him, its mandibles snapping shut just inches from his face. Ivanov managed to fire a shot into its eye, but the creature didn't fall. It reared back, ready to strike again, but before it could, one of Ivanov's men threw a grenade, the explosion ripping the creature apart.

Ivanov quickly grabbed the injured woman, carrying her to safety as his men covered their retreat. They made it to an armored vehicle, and the civilians quickly loaded inside. As they sped away, Ivanov looked back at the burning city, knowing that this battle was far from over. The creatures were relentless, and they were running out of time.

Sydney, Australia
Wednesday 07:43 PM

Meanwhile, in Sydney, the creatures were different still. They were grotesque amalgamations of human and animal features; their bodies twisted and malformed in ways that defied logic. One of the most horrifying was a creature that had once been a man but had been fused with something else—its body elongated, its limbs distorted, and its face a horrific blend of human and something aquatic, with eyes that bulged out of its skull and a mouth filled with razor-sharp teeth as it propped itself out of the water.

The city's defenses had crumbled under the onslaught, and the people of Sydney had taken matters into their own hands. Armed mobs roamed the streets, hunting down the creatures wherever they could find them. The city had become a battleground, with every man, woman, and child fighting for their survival.

One such group had taken refuge in the Sydney Opera House, fortifying the iconic building as best they could. They had barricaded the entrances, set traps, and armed themselves with whatever weapons they could find. Among them was a police officer, Sarah Smith, who had taken on the role of leader.

She stood at the entrance, her shotgun at the ready, as the creatures began to approach. They moved with a strange, jerking gait, their twisted forms barely recognizable as human. Sarah could see the fear in the eyes of the people around her, but she knew that they had no choice but to fight.

"Hold your ground!" she called out, her voice steady despite the fear gnawing at her insides. "We can't let them get inside!"

Without thinking twice, she fired, hitting some square in the head. Her bravery got the others to follow suit. Armed with rifles and guns meant to fend off Kangaroos or other pests, they did not hesitate to open fire. As the creatures fell, one remained alive.

The semi-aquatic andromorph growled at them. The bullets had grazed multiple parts of its slippery, slimy body, but it was very much alive. Just when it was about to lunge forward, one of the younger people fired a flare gun at it. It wasn't the gun but rather the smoke that made it stumble backward, giving another member the time to take aim and fire.

Though the bullet hit its target and the beast toppled back into the water, they knew that it wasn't dead…but now, they were expecting it.

Osaka, Japan

Tuesday 08:43 PM

The ancient city of temples and tradition bore witness to a battle that was one of eerie silence. The sun had set hours ago, but the streets were bathed in an unnatural, otherworldly glow. Shadows twisted and elongated in impossible ways, and the air hummed with a low, sinister frequency that vibrated deep within the bones.

The creature that emerged in the city was unlike anything anyone had ever seen. It was humanoid in shape, but its body was covered in glistening black scales that absorbed light rather than reflected it. Its head was featureless, a smooth, oval dome with no eyes, nose, or mouth. Long, spindly arms ended in clawed hands that seemed to drip with a dark, viscous fluid.

The Self-Defense Forces had set up a perimeter around the creature, using the narrow streets to their advantage to limit its movement. Snipers were positioned on rooftops, their scopes trained on the entity as it glided silently through the city.

"Hold your fire!" Captain Nakamura ordered, his voice steady despite the tension. "We need to see how it reacts before we engage."

But the creature showed no signs of aggression. It moved slowly, deliberately, as if searching for something. Civilians who had failed to evacuate watched in horror as the creature passed by, its presence causing an overwhelming sense of dread that left them paralyzed. One young man, overcome by fear, attempted to flee, but as he ran, the creature's head snapped in his direction.

It moved faster than anyone could have anticipated. In a blur of motion, it closed the distance and reached out with one clawed hand.

The young man screamed as the claws pierced his flesh, but his voice was quickly silenced. The creature lifted him effortlessly, and as it held him aloft, the fluid dripping from its claws began to seep into his body. The man convulsed violently, his skin turning black and his eyes rolling back into his head. Within moments, he was reduced to nothing more than a desiccated husk, which the creature discarded without a second thought.

Captain Nakamura gave the order to fire, and the silence was shattered by the sound of gunshots. But the bullets seemed to have little effect. The creature continued its slow, methodical search, seemingly indifferent to the soldiers' efforts.

Realizing that conventional weapons were useless, Nakamura made a difficult decision. "Fall back," he ordered. "We can't stop it. All we can do is contain it."

As the soldiers retreated, they left behind a city that was forever changed. The creature continued its search, moving deeper into Osaka, leaving behind a trail of death and despair.

Cholistan, Pakistan
Thursday 03:43 PM

In the vast emptiness of the Cholistan Desert, another encounter was unfolding. Here, the landscape was as alien as the creature that had appeared. The creature was a nasty hybrid of man and insect, with a chitinous exoskeleton that shimmered in the harsh moonlight. Its body was elongated, with multiple jointed legs that allowed it to scuttle across the sand with frightening speed. Its head was vaguely humanoid, but its eyes were compound, like those of a fly, and its mouth was a gaping maw lined with razor-sharp mandibles.

A structured team of military personnel had been sent to investigate reports of a strange phenomenon in the desert, but they were unprepared for what they found. The creature had made its nest in an abandoned outpost, its presence warping the environment around it. The air stank with the smell of decay, and the sand had taken on a sickly green color as if poisoned by the creature's presence.

"Stay sharp," young yet trained Lieutenant Arslan whispered, his voice barely audible over the wind. "We don't know what we're dealing with here."

The team advanced cautiously, their weapons trained on the entrance to the outpost. As they approached, the creature burst forth from its nest, moving with blinding speed. The soldiers opened fire, but the creature's exoskeleton deflected the bullets with ease. It lunged at them, its mandibles snapping shut with a sickening crunch as it caught one of the men in its jaws.

The soldier screamed as he was lifted into the air, his body convulsing as the creature injected a paralyzing venom into his bloodstream. The others could only watch in horror as their comrade was slowly consumed, his flesh and bone crushed by the creature's powerful jaws.

The team watched in horror as the creature devoured their comrade, its mouthpieces dripping with blood. The soldier's screams were abruptly cut off, leaving only the sound of the wind and the chittering of the monstrous hybrid. The Lieutenant knew they couldn't keep firing aimlessly. The creature's exoskeleton was too tough for conventional bullets, and its speed made it nearly impossible to target its weak points.

"Fall back!" he commanded, his voice steady despite the chaos. "We need to draw it out—get it into open ground!"

The remaining soldiers obeyed, retreating towards the clearing where the desert met the outpost. The creature pursued them, its many legs skittering over the sand with terrifying speed. As they reached the open ground, Arslan noticed the faint glow of dawn on the horizon. They needed to end this before the creature took out the entire squad.

"Form a perimeter!" the Lieutenant ordered, quickly assessing the situation. "Aim for the joints in its legs. We slow it down, then we go for the eyes."

The soldiers spread out in a rough circle, their weapons trained on the advancing creature. Arslan knew they had one chance—if they could cripple its legs, they might have enough time to deliver a fatal blow.

"Now!" he shouted.

The soldiers opened fire, concentrating their shots on the creature's legs. This time, the bullets found their mark, piercing the thinner joints between the chitinous plates. The creature shrieked a high-pitched sound that set the soldiers' nerves on edge. It stumbled, its movement becoming erratic as it tried to balance on its wounded legs.

Arslan took the opportunity to signal two men to flank the creature while the others kept it distracted. As the soldiers on the flanks moved in, one of them was caught by a sweeping limb and thrown violently against a rock, his body crumpling on impact. Another soldier, attempting to close in, was impaled by the creature's sharp jawbones, his blood spraying across the sand.

"Keep it distracted!" Arslan yelled, his voice hoarse with strain.

With only two soldiers left, The Lieutenant knew they had to act quickly. He sprinted towards the creature's side, his heart pounding as he aimed his rifle at one of its compound eyes. With a steady hand, he squeezed the trigger, sending a burst of bullets into the creature's vulnerable eye.

The creature recoiled, its movements becoming frantic and disoriented as it lost its depth perception. Arslan fired again, this time at the other eye, blinding it completely. The creature thrashed wildly, its legs giving out as it succumbed to its injuries.

Arslan stood over the dying creature, his chest heaving with exertion. He had lost four men, good men who had fought bravely against an enemy they had never imagined. As the first light of dawn broke over the horizon, he muttered a final prayer for his fallen comrades, hoping their sacrifice had not been in vain.

The news of what had occurred in the Ukrainian bunker traveled quickly, and within minutes, the communication line to Fort Blackwood in the Rocky Mountains was buzzing with the latest update. John Harrows, who had been going over tactical plans with his team, listened intently as the complaint was relayed to him. His expression hardened as the details were laid out, his disapproval clear.

"She's compromised," Harrows said flatly, his voice carrying a note of finality. "This isn't some academic exercise. We're dealing with things that could wipe us out if we're not careful. Nadia Ayoub is too emotionally involved, and that's a liability we can't afford. She needs to be taken off the case immediately."

Marcus Flynn, who had been standing nearby, shot Harrows a look of incredulous disbelief. "You can't be serious, John. The kid's got her heart in this, working day and night. If you take her off the case now, we'll lose valuable time. Shaw said she's the one who's been working closest with these entities; she knows them better than anyone."

Harrows' eyes narrowed. "Diligence doesn't mean anything if she's going to get people killed, Marcus. Her methods are unorthodox and dangerous. This is about survival."

Marcus bristled, his frustration boiling over. "We're not going to survive if we start pulling people off the project every time they try something different! Nadia is getting results, and if you push her out now, we'll be set back weeks, maybe months!"

The tension between the two men was palpable, the argument escalating as Major General Whitmore watched from his position at the head of the table. His patience, already thin from the pressures of their mission, snapped.

"Enough!" Whitmore's voice thundered through the room, silencing both Harrows and Marcus instantly. The general's eyes blazed with authority as he glared at them. "I don't care if she's goddamn Lady Liberty; if she's a liability, she's out. Now hold your tongues and stop acting like you got your fannies in a twist!"

Before either man could respond, a young cadet entered the room, his face pale and his hands shaking slightly as he handed Whitmore a stack of reports. "Sir, these just came in. They... they're from the outside world, sir. Things are... they're not looking good."

Whitmore snatched the reports from the cadet's hands, his eyes scanning the pages quickly. His expression grew darker with each word, his jaw tightening as he read aloud the most critical updates.

"Dimensional breaches have escalated," Whitmore began, his voice grim. "There are reports of entire regions destabilizing. Massive storms appearing out of nowhere, hurricanes forming over land, and earthquakes in places where there's no fault line. It's like the laws of nature are breaking down."

He paused, flipping to another page. "Multiple sightings of unidentified entities—large, grotesque creatures materializing in populated areas. Civilian casualties are in the thousands, and it's spreading faster than we can contain it. The Atlantic coast is being hit the hardest. Cities like Boston, New York, and Washington, D.C. are reporting mass evacuations, but there's chaos everywhere. The military is stretched thin just trying to maintain order."

The cadet's voice trembled as he added, "Sir, there's more. There's evidence that these breaches are becoming permanent. Once they open, they're not closing. And the things…they just…God, they just keep coming and coming."

The room fell into a stunned silence, the weight of the cadet's words hanging heavy in the air. Marcus felt a cold dread settle in his stomach, the enormity of the situation finally hitting home. This was bigger than anything they had imagined, and it was getting worse by the minute.

Whitmore slammed the reports down on the table, his gaze sweeping over the men in the room. "We don't have time for debates or second-guessing. We need solutions, and we need them now. If that means pulling people off the project, so be it. If it means taking risks, then we take them. But I'll be damned if I let this thing tear our world apart while we stand around bickering like children."

His words were like a slap to the face, jolting everyone in the room back to reality. The severity of the crisis left no room for hesitation. As the team scrambled to respond, the stakes of their mission had never been clearer—or more terrifying.

* * *

A few hours later, the dimly lit war room at Fort Blackwood buzzed with activity. Maps, digital screens, and tactical layouts filled the walls, casting an eerie blue glow over the gathering of soldiers, strategists, and commanders. Major General Samuel Whitmore stood at the head of the table, his stern face illuminated by the flickering lights. Across from him, John Harrows reviewed a series of reports, his expression grim.

The news had just come in—critical intel on the cabal's whereabouts in Switzerland. But the information was a double-edged sword; while it presented an opportunity, it also required immediate action, even as the threat of otherworldly creatures loomed over them.

Harrows took a deep breath, his mind racing as he considered the situation. "Gentlemen," he began, addressing the room. "We have less than six hours until the shipment of weapons arrives from the bunker. This gives us a tight window to prepare for both the immediate threats and a potential strike on the cabal."

Major General Whitmore nodded. "We need to divide our focus—ensure that our defenses here are ready while also planning for a surgical strike in Switzerland. Let's break down our strategy."

Harrows gestured to a large digital map of the surrounding area. "Based on the reports we've received, the creatures we're dealing with have various weaknesses. For instance, the creature referred to as 'Eye Sore' is vulnerable to high-frequency sonic waves. The symbiotic entities are susceptible to extreme temperatures, and the insectoid creature we heard about from Pakistan appears to be weak against rapid-fire weapons designed to penetrate chitinous armor."

He pointed to specific locations on the map. "We'll set up perimeter defenses at these key points. Sonic emitters will be placed at the north and east gates—if 'Eye Sore' or similar entities approach, we can drive them back or incapacitate them. Flamethrowers and liquid nitrogen sprayers will be stationed along the southern ridge to counter any symbiotic entities. Lastly, we'll reinforce the bunkers with rapid-fire turrets that are specifically designed to pierce heavy armor."

Whitmore tapped the map thoughtfully. "What about the soldiers on the ground? We need to ensure they're equipped with the right gear."

Harrows nodded. "The new armor prototypes we're receiving are specifically designed to offer resistance against parasitic attacks and acid burns—two of the most common forms of damage these creatures can inflict. We'll also distribute specialized weapons—plasma rifles, cryo-grenades, and EMP devices to disrupt the nervous systems of any mechanical or partially mechanical entities."

As they solidified the defense strategies, Harrows received a message from Phoenix. He glanced at his phone, the cryptic text confirming that Phoenix had managed to secure critical intel on the cabal. Dr. Anya Petrova, an insider at New Dawn, had pinpointed Dr. Weiss' location to a remote mountain lodge in Switzerland. The timing was perfect, but it required immediate action.

Harrows cleared his throat and addressed the room again. "I've just received an update from my source—Dr. Weiss and key cabal members are holding a physical meeting at a mountain lodge in Switzerland. This is our chance to strike, but we need to do it covertly. We can't afford to attract too much attention or risk the cabal fleeing before we arrive."

Whitmore's eyes narrowed. "What's your plan?"

"We'll deploy a small, elite team equipped with cloaking technology from New Dawn. These operatives will be inserted via helicopter a few kilometers away from the lodge to avoid detection. They'll move under cover in darkness, using the terrain to their advantage. The mission is twofold—eliminate high-value targets and secure any intel they may have on their future plans."

He paused, then added, "Simultaneously, we'll launch a cyber-attack to disrupt their communications. Shade, another of our assets, has already intercepted some of their digital traffic. We'll use this to create a diversion, making them believe their systems are compromised from within, causing confusion and lowering their defenses."

Just as Harrows finished outlining the Switzerland operation, Marcus Flynn, standing by the comms terminal, received an intermission from Shade. His eyes widened as the message played out—a match for Helena Voss's head of security had been found near the mountain lodge. This was the confirmation they needed.

"Harrows," Marcus called out, interrupting the discussion. "My guy just confirmed Helena Voss' security detail has been spotted near the lodge. She's there."

Harrows turned, his expression serious. "That changes things. We can't miss this chance. Voss is a key player and owns both the means and the lack of a heart to bring the world to an end for power. If we can capture or eliminate her, it could cripple the cabal's operations."

Whitmore crossed his arms. "This just got a lot riskier. We need a contingency plan. If Voss escapes—"

"She won't," Harrows interrupted with his voice firm. "But if she does, we'll have a backup team ready to intercept her on the roads out of the area. We'll set up roadblocks disguised as local military exercises. If she tries to flee, we'll catch her."

Whitmore's stern face softened slightly. "It's risky, but it might work. Let's get to work, gentlemen. We've got a lot to do and not much time to do it."

As the meeting wrapped up, it was becoming clearer by the minute- the fate of not just Fort Blackwood but potentially the entire world hung in the balance. The soldiers and strategists dispersed to their stations, each man and woman preparing for the fight of their lives, knowing that the hours ahead would determine the future of their world.

Chapter 7: Convergence

The luxury mountain lodge stood tall and imposing against the backdrop of the Swiss Alps. Its sleek modern design was vastly different from the ancient, almost eldritch energy that permeated the area. The night was unnaturally still as if the very air held its breath in anticipation of the horrors that were about to unfold. A full moon hung low in the sky, its cold light casting long, eerie shadows across the rooftop where the real nightmare was about to begin.

Helena Voss, draped in an elegant red cloak, stood at the edge of the rooftop, her eyes gleaming with a mix of excitement and malevolence. She was the orchestrator of this dark symphony, the puppet master pulling the strings of an ancient power that had been dormant for far too long. Behind her, the advanced and stable version of the Large Hadron Collider (LHC) hummed with a low, ominous vibration. This was no ordinary collider—it was a doorway, a deliberate portal to realms that should have remained untouched.

Around the collider, a circle of unnerving statues loomed each one a grotesque representation of otherworldly deities, their forms twisted and alien. The statues seemed to pulse with a life of their own, their empty eyes staring out into the void as if waiting for something— or someone—to answer their silent call. These were the gods the Cabal worshipped, entities from dimensions beyond human comprehension, beings of unimaginable power and malice.

Dr. Weiss, standing near the control panel, was focused, his fingers hovering over the buttons that would activate the collider. He was a man of science, yet tonight, he was a sorcerer, ready to summon forces that had been long forgotten by the world of men. He turned to Helena, his voice steady but charged with anticipation. "Are you ready, Ms. Voss?"

Helena smiled with a cold, calculated expression that sent shivers down the spines of the few cult members who dared to glance her way. "Do it," she commanded, her voice like ice.

Weiss pressed the final sequence of buttons, and the collider roared to life. The rooftop seemed to tremble as the machine accelerated, its energy building into a crescendo. The statues around the collider began to glow, their once-stone surfaces now alive with a sinister light that matched the full moon above.

As the energy peaked, a rift began to tear open in the sky above the lodge. It was as if the very fabric of reality was being ripped apart, revealing a gaping maw of darkness beyond. From this void, a horde of locust-like creatures swarmed out, their wings buzzing with a deafening hum as they filled the night air. These were not ordinary locusts—each was the size of a human hand, their bodies covered in sharp, metallic exoskeletons that glinted in the moonlight. Their eyes burned with an unnatural red glow, and their mandibles clicked hungrily as they poured out of the portal in an unending stream.

The Cabal members watched in awe, their faces lit by the hellish light of the portal. But the horror was only beginning. As the last of the locusts emerged, a massive eye appeared in the portal. It was impossibly large, filling the sky with its cold, unblinking gaze. The eye was ancient, its iris a swirling vortex of colors that defied description. It looked down upon the world with an intelligence and malice that was beyond human understanding.

For a moment, the eye simply stared as if weighing the worth of the beings below. The Cabal members felt a collective shudder run through them, the primal fear of being watched by something far greater, far more powerful than themselves. But the eye made no move to enter the world—perhaps it was waiting, or perhaps it was simply content to observe, its presence a reminder that they were but insects in the grand scheme of the cosmos.

Helena Voss stepped forward, raising her arms as if in greeting to the eye. "Behold!" she called out, her voice ringing with triumph. "We have opened the way! We are your servants, your vessels in this world!"

But the eye gave no response, its gaze cold and indifferent. The locusts continued to swarm, and the statues around the collider seemed to pulse with greater intensity as if feeding off the energy of the portal.

Dr. Weiss remained at the control panel, his face pale but resolute. This was what he had worked for, sacrificed for—a chance to stand on the precipice of a new age, to witness the dawn of a world reshaped by forces beyond imagination. Yet, as he looked up at the massive eye in the sky, a sliver of doubt crept into his mind. Had they truly harnessed this power, or had they merely unleashed something that could never be controlled?

The night wore on, the moon hanging like a silent witness to the dark ritual unfolding below. The portal remained open, its connection to the other dimension growing stronger with each passing moment. The eye continued to watch, its presence a heavy, oppressive force that bore down on all who stood beneath it.

Helena Voss lowered her arms, a satisfied smile playing on her lips. The door had been opened; the way cleared. Now, it was only a matter of time before the true power of the Cabal was unleashed upon the world. And when that day came, she would stand at the forefront, a queen of the new order, with the gods of the abyss as her allies.

But for now, the eye watched, and the mountains trembled beneath its gaze.

***

The atmosphere inside Fort Blackwood was thick with tension and anticipation. The soldiers moved with purpose, their faces set in grim determination as they suited up in the newly arrived armor. The shipment from the bunker had finally arrived just minutes ago, and the soldiers wasted no time donning the state-of-the-art gear that could very well be their last line of defense against the horrors awaiting them.

The armor was unlike anything they had ever seen before, a blend of cutting-edge technology and otherworldly design. The exoskeleton was sleek and form-fitting, made from a composite material that was as light as it was durable. The surface of the armor shimmered with a dark, iridescent sheen, reflecting the dim lights of the hangar-like oil on water. Each suit was custom-fitted and molded to the individual soldier's body to allow maximum mobility without sacrificing protection.

Embedded within the armor were advanced systems designed to counter the various threats they might face. Heat resistance was achieved through a series of cooling vents that dispersed excess heat away from the body while a layer of insulating material provided protection against extreme temperatures. Electricity resistance came from an intricate network of conductive fibers woven into the suit, capable of dissipating electrical shocks before they could reach the wearer. Water resistance was ensured by a hydrophobic coating that repelled moisture, allowing the soldiers to operate in wet environments without the fear of shorting out their gear.

Harrows, always one to lead from the front, was in the midst of suiting up alongside his men. His suit was slightly bulkier than the others, customized with additional plating to protect against more powerful attacks. The helmet, with its sleek visor, was equipped with a heads-up display (HUD) that provided real-time data on the battlefield, including enemy positions, vitals, and environmental conditions. The HUD also linked directly to the communication network, ensuring that Harrows could stay in constant contact with his team.

As he secured the final pieces of his armor, Harrows couldn't help but feel the weight of the moment. They were about to embark on a mission that could very well determine the fate of the world, and he knew that the stakes had never been higher. He flexed his fingers, feeling the responsive material of the gloves conform to his movements. This was it—the culmination of all their training, all their preparations. Now, it was time to face the unknown.

The soldiers, now fully suited up, made their way to the military transport plane that would take them to Switzerland. The plane was a massive, heavily modified C-130 designed to carry both troops and equipment into hostile territory. The interior was a stark, utilitarian space, with rows of seats along the walls and racks of weapons and gear lining the aisles. The soldiers took their seats, the hum of the engines filling the cabin as they prepared for take-off.

Harrows settled into his seat, securing his harness as the plane began to taxi down the runway. The weight of the armor was comforting, a reminder of the protection it offered, but it did little to ease the tension in the air. The soldiers around him were silent, each lost in their thoughts as they steeled themselves for the battle to come.

Just as the plane lifted off the ground, Harrows' comm system crackled to life. It was Marcus, his voice calm but carrying an edge of his usual sarcasm. "Harrows, I've got a message for you from Phoenix."

Harrows raised an eyebrow, intrigued. "Go ahead."

There was a brief pause, and then Marcus spoke again, his tone clearly amused. "They said... 'Do not get killed.'"

Harrows couldn't help but let out a dry chuckle. "Tell Phoenix I'll do my best. Or better yet, establish an audio connection to me directly."

But as he ended the transmission, Harrows knew that the message was more than just a reminder to stay alive. It was a warning— whatever they were about to face in Switzerland was beyond anything they had encountered before. The Cabal, the creatures, the portal— it all pointed to a threat that defied comprehension, and survival was far from guaranteed.

The plane continued its ascent, breaking through the clouds as it set a course for Switzerland. Below them, the world was shrouded in darkness, the moon a cold sentinel watching over the unfolding chaos. Harrows looked out at the night sky, his thoughts turning to the ritual they were about to interrupt. He could only hope that they were prepared for whatever awaited them on that mountain.

The cabin lights dimmed, signaling the start of the long flight ahead. The soldiers around Harrows began to close their eyes, trying to catch some rest before the battle. But Harrows remained awake, his mind racing with thoughts of strategy, of the enemy they were about to face, and of the cryptic message from Phoenix.

Do not get killed.

It was easier said than done. But Harrows was nothing if not determined. Whatever awaited them in Switzerland, he would face it head-on, and he would bring his men back alive—if it was the last thing he did.

After an agonizing few hours, the military transport plane descended through the cloud cover, the jagged peaks of the Swiss Alps looming below. The luxury mountain lodge, a remote and heavily guarded fortress nestled high in the mountains, was their target. The night was eerily quiet, the only sound the low hum of the plane's engines as it approached the drop zone.

Inside the plane, Harrows and his team made final preparations. The atmosphere was tense, every soldier fully aware of the danger that awaited them. The intelligence from Phoenix had been clear—the Cabal was performing a ritual at the lodge, using an advanced and stable version of the LHC to open a deliberate portal to another dimension. The stakes couldn't be higher.

Harrows stood at the front of the cabin, addressing his team. "Listen up, everyone. This isn't just another mission. What we're about to face is beyond anything we've encountered. We've got intel on the Cabal's location and their ritual. Our objective is to stop that portal from opening completely. Take out any hostiles, but the priority is to disrupt the ritual and shut down their LHC. Stay sharp, stay alive. Let's move."

The soldiers nodded, their expressions hidden behind their visors but their resolve clear. The back of the plane opened with a hydraulic hiss, revealing the dark, snow-covered landscape below. One by one, the soldiers jumped, their black parachutes unfurling as they descended silently toward the lodge.

Harrows landed first, his feet crunching softly in the snow. The lodge was visible in the distance, an imposing structure with tall, angular architecture that seemed to meld with the mountain itself. He signaled for his team to spread out and advance cautiously. The wind whipped around them, carrying the distant echoes of chanting from the lodge—a rhythmic, unsettling sound that set their nerves on edge.

They moved swiftly through the snow, using the natural cover of the rocks and trees to conceal their approach. As they neared the lodge, Harrows held up a fist, signaling the team to stop. He peered through the scope of his rifle, scanning the area. The Cabal's security forces were patrolling the perimeter, heavily armed and alert. These weren't just ordinary guards—they moved with the precision and discipline of trained soldiers.

Harrows whispered into his comms, "We've got hostiles on the perimeter. Take them out quietly. No alarms."

The soldiers split into pairs, each taking up a position to neutralize the guards. Harrows and his partner, Sergeant Daniels, crept closer to a pair of guards near the entrance. With silent precision, they synchronized their attack—Harrows shot the first guard with a suppressed round to the head, while Daniels dispatched the second with a swift knife strike to the throat. The bodies fell silently into the snow.

"Perimeter clear," Harrows whispered. "Move in."

The team converged on the lodge, regrouping at the main entrance. Harrows checked the schematics of the building on his HUD. "The LHC is on the rooftop. We need to move fast. Split into two teams. Team One, secure the ground floor and cut off any reinforcements. Team Two, with me—we're heading for the roof."

Team One breached the entrance, moving with tactical precision as they cleared the ground floor. The sound of suppressed gunfire echoed through the halls as they took down the remaining guards. Meanwhile, Harrows led Team Two up the grand staircase, moving quickly but cautiously. The chanting grew louder as they ascended, the eerie rhythm reverberating through the walls.

They reached the rooftop door, where Harrows paused. "Get ready. We don't know what we're walking into."

He kicked the door open, and they stormed onto the rooftop. The sight that greeted them was surreal. The advanced LHC, a massive circular structure glowing with an unnatural light, was positioned at the center of the roof. Around it stood several Cabal members, their faces obscured by dark hoods, chanting in unison as the machine hummed with energy. Surrounding the LHC were grotesque statues of ancient deities, their forms twisted and disturbing, watching over the ritual with lifeless eyes.

Above them, the portal had already begun to open—a swirling vortex of darkness and light that seemed to tear at the fabric of reality itself. From within the portal, a horde of locust-like creatures poured out, their wings buzzing ominously as they filled the sky. A massive eye, monstrous and alien, peeked through the portal, observing the scene below with a malevolent intelligence.

"Engage!" Harrows shouted, and the rooftop erupted into madness.

The soldiers opened fire, their bullets ripping through the air as they targeted the Cabal members. The Cabalists fought back with ferocity, using conventional weapons while the swarms of locust-like creatures, twisted and monstrous, poured out of the vortex, their buzzing filling the night air as they, too, descended upon the soldiers.

"Steady, men!" Harrows shouted. The soldiers continued to launch a barrage of bullets, cutting through the swarm. But for every creature that fell, ten more seemed to take its place. The soldiers fought valiantly, their advanced armor holding up against the onslaught, but it was clear that the swarm was relentless.

Amidst the chaos, Harrows spotted movement near the LHC. Helena Voss, the powerful and enigmatic business executive and a prominent member of the Cabal, stood with Dr. Weiss. Her expression was one of cold determination; her eyes glinted with a malevolent light, and her billowing dark robes only added to the mysterious persona. Dr. Weiss, in contrast, looked more calculating, his mind clearly racing as he observed the battlefield.

"You can't stop this," Helena Voss called out, her voice carrying over the wind. "This is only the beginning. The portal will open fully, and we will harness its power. You and your pitiful soldiers are nothing but insects to be crushed."

Harrows gritted his teeth and signaled for his team to advance. "We'll see about that, Voss. You underestimate us."

As they moved closer, one of the soldiers, Sergeant Diaz, suddenly cried out as a locust creature latched onto his armor, its razor-sharp mandibles tearing at the reinforced plating. Without hesitation, Diaz ripped the creature off and crushed it underfoot, but the damage was done—his suit's systems were compromised, and he knew he wouldn't last long in the fight.

"Go! I'll cover you!" Diaz shouted to the others, his voice strained but resolute. He unleashed a barrage of gunfire, taking out as many creatures as he could, buying his comrades precious time to reach the LHC. Harrows gave Diaz a grim nod, knowing that his sacrifice would not be in vain.

The soldiers pushed forward, but as they neared the LHC, Dr. Weiss stepped in front of them, holding a small device in his hand. "Not so fast, gents," he sneered. "This technology is far beyond your understanding."

He activated the device, and a shimmering energy field sprang up around the LHC, repelling the soldiers and deflecting their bullets. Harrows cursed under his breath. They needed a different approach—one that combined their limited knowledge of both science and the occult.

"Phoenix, I need your help!" Harrows called out into his comms, knowing that Phoenix, the mysterious hacker who had provided them with crucial intel, was monitoring the situation. "We need to break this field."

"Working on it," Phoenix replied through the voice-changing device they were using. "There's a way to disrupt the energy field, but it's going to require some serious coordination. You'll need to disable the LHC's core stabilizers. They're located around the base of the machine; heavily protected."

Harrows relayed the information to his team. "Jenkins, get to the stabilizers. We'll cover you."

As Jenkins moved toward the stabilizers, Helena Voss raised her arms, chanting in an ancient language. The air around her crackled with dark energy, and bolts of lightning began to strike the rooftop, targeting the soldiers. One bolt struck Sergeant Daniels, sending him sprawling to the ground, his armor smoking. Another soldier was hit moments later, his screams cut short as he fell lifelessly to the ground.

Harrows knew they were running out of time. The portal was growing larger by the second, and the swarm of creatures was intensifying. He made a split-second decision. "I'm going after Voss. The rest of you, keep those creatures off Jenkins!"

He charged toward Voss, dodging the lightning bolts as best he could. As he closed the distance, she turned to face him, a cruel smile playing on her lips. "You're a fool. This power is beyond you."

"Maybe," Harrows replied, "but I've got something you don't—a team willing to lay down their lives to stop you."

With that, he lunged at her, tackling her to the ground. As they struggled, her hands glowed with dark energy, crackling sounds filling the air as she tried to unleash a spell. But Harrows was relentless, using his sheer physical strength to overpower her. He grabbed her by the throat, slamming her head against the cold stone rooftop, and for a brief moment, the dark energy flickered and dissipated. It was frightening to see how despite the impact on her head and the pressure on her windpipe…she was still kicking and moving.

Meanwhile, Jenkins reached the stabilizers and began planting explosives around them. The soldiers fought valiantly against the swarm, but their numbers were dwindling. Just as Jenkins finished setting the charges, a bolt of lightning struck him, sending him flying back. His armor absorbed most of the impact, but he was gravely injured.

"Jenkins, detonate the charges!" Harrows shouted, still grappling with Voss.

Jenkins, struggling to move, reached for the detonator. He looked up at Harrows, knowing this might be his last act. "It's been an honor, sir," he said, his voice weak but determined.

He pressed the detonator, and the charges exploded with a deafening roar. The stabilizers shattered, sending a wave of energy through the LHC. The protective field around the machine flickered and then collapsed entirely. The LHC itself began to destabilize, the glow around it pulsing erratically.

Voss gasped for air, her dark eyes burning with hatred. "You may have stopped this ritual," she hissed, "but you haven't won. The Cabal is far more powerful than you can imagine."

"Maybe so," Harrows said coldly, "but at least tonight, we're taking you down."

Before Voss could utter another word, Harrows drew his sidearm and fired, ending her life with a single shot.

The rooftop was in chaos. The soldiers, battered and bruised, regrouped around the LHC. Dr. Weiss, seeing that the ritual had failed and the portal was closing, attempted to flee, but Harrows shot him in the leg, bringing him down.

"You're not going anywhere," Harrows declared, standing over Weiss. "This ends now."

The LHC began to overload, the unstable energy threatening to tear the rooftop apart. "Fall back!" Harrows ordered. "We need to get out of here before this thing blows."

As the soldiers retreated, Harrows caught sight of Jenkins, still lying near the stabilizers, barely conscious. He rushed over and dragged Jenkins to his feet, half-carrying, half-dragging him away from the collapsing machine.

Just then, Weiss called out to the Eye above in a language that none of them understood. And as Harrows was about to aim and fire at his arm the eye in the portal shifted, allowing tendrils of smoke to snake out. The soldiers backed up as the tentacles gained density and coiled around Weiss. Just as they thought he was a goner, they yanked him above the ground, pulling him through the gateway in the clouds.

With the LHC about to explode, Harrows and his team made a desperate run for the staircase. Just as they reached it, the machine detonated, the shockwave sending them tumbling down the steps.

The explosion lit up the night sky, a beacon of their victory amidst the carnage.

The portal was sealed, and the ritual was disrupted, but at a heavy cost. The soldiers who had fallen, the sacrifices made—it was a somber reminder of the price of war against the darkness. But for now, they had bought the world some time, delaying the Cabal's plans.

As they regrouped in the relative safety of the staircase, Harrows took a moment to catch his breath. The air was thick with the acrid smell of smoke and ozone, remnants of the violent clash that had just transpired on the rooftop. They had won, but the cost was evident in the empty spaces where their comrades once stood.

As Harrows stared at the spot where Jenkins would've stood if he were still alive, guilt gnawed at him. He had tried to pull Jenkins' body to safety before the explosion, but everything had happened too quickly. The explosion had ripped through the LHC, and he knew, in that split second, that Jenkins was a goner. Now, the silence that followed the chaos was almost unbearable.

The comms in Harrows' ear crackled to life, pulling him from his thoughts. Major General Whitmore's voice came through, sharp and commanding despite the underlying tension. "Harrows, listen up. We've got a new problem. Satellite imagery has confirmed a massive entity, a fire giant of sorts, moving toward Russia. The cold waters of the Arctic are slowing it down, but it's still coming. This thing is a threat to anything in its path."

Harrows closed his eyes for a moment, taking in the grim news. His men, what was left of them, were in no condition to face another battle, let alone against a titan of fire. Yet, there was no room for hesitation. The world was falling apart, and there was no place for rest. "Understood, Sam," Harrows replied, his voice steady. "We'll return to Fort Blackwood and regroup."

He looked around at his team, their faces darkened by soot and streaked with sweat. These were the survivors, those who had lived through hell on that rooftop. He saw the fatigue in their eyes, the weight of loss, and the determination to keep fighting, no matter the odds. They were soldiers, after all, and they knew their duty.

Harrows forced himself to stand, his muscles protesting with every movement. "We're heading back to Fort Blackwood," he announced, his voice carrying over the wind.

As he spoke, he couldn't help but think of Jenkins again. The man had given everything, and now he was gone, just another name on a long list of the fallen. Harrows pushed the grief aside; there would be time to mourn later if there was a later.

Once Whitmore was out, Harrows and his men were once more alone in the cold, desolate aftermath of their battle. The next phase was coming, and it would be just as deadly, if not more so. But for now, they would return to Fort Blackwood, rest, and prepare for whatever horrors awaited them.

He looked at his men, giving them a nod of encouragement, even though his own heart was heavy with doubt. They had fought and bled together, and they would continue to do so until the very end.

"Let's move out," he ordered, and with that, the soldiers began their descent from the mountain, their eyes set on the horizon, where a new and terrible threat awaited them.

Meanwhile, at the Fort, the comms clicked off, and Whitmore turned to see Marcus Flynn, sitting a few steps away, petting Max, Harrows' loyal dog. Max was a comforting presence in the mayhem. It was Phoenix who had informed him of the titan's impending approach, and Marcus was already on the move, reaching out to the bunker's team for any possible solutions.

"Thomas, it's Marcus," he spoke into the video call, his tone urgent. Whitmore's eyes narrowed at his audacity. "We need to know if you've got anything we can use remotely. Drones, missiles, tanks — whatever can be controlled from afar. We need firepower and we need it now. There's a new threat. Russia's in trouble, and we can't let them go down in flames."

As Marcus awaited a response, his gaze shifted to Shade, the hacker who had been their unseen ally in this war. This was Marcus' first time seeing Shade, and honestly, he could see why Nadia had called him creepy.

"Shade, I need you to pinpoint that Titan's exact location. Use the satellite imagery and get me coordinates. We need to know where it's headed."

Shade did not speak; his eyes moved to another screen, and he nodded, fingers already moving on the keyboard.

Finally, Marcus turned his attention back to Whitmore, his expression one of grim determination. He spoke with as much respect as he could muster, but the gravity of the situation was clear in his words. "General, you need to get in touch with the Russians officially. This isn't about borders anymore. We're all in this together — every man, woman, and child against something that wants to wipe us out. We can't let that thing reach the shore."

There was a moment of silence as Whitmore considered the words. The general had seen his fair share of conflicts, but this was different. The enemy wasn't another country; it was something beyond comprehension. "I'll make the call," Whitmore finally replied. "But you better be ready for what comes next."

* * *

The low hum of the bunker's ventilation system was the only sound breaking the silence in the massive underground operations room. The concrete walls, lined with state-of-the-art equipment, seemed to close in on the technicians as they moved with a sense of urgency. Thomas, the ever-enthusiastic and vibrant technician with a sharp mind and steady hands, supervised the cadets as they placed the latest drones and missiles onto the launch pads.

Each drone was a marvel of modern engineering, equipped with high-precision targeting systems and advanced AI to navigate the most treacherous battlefields. The missiles, sleek and deadly, were armed with warheads capable of delivering devastating blows to even the most formidable foes. The cadets, young and still green in the art of war, followed Thomas' instructions with a mixture of fear and determination.

"Careful with that one," Thomas said, his voice carrying a note of authority as he watched a cadet handle one of the more temperamental drones. "You break it, and we're down one more weapon against those things."

The cadet nodded nervously, making sure to secure the drone in place with delicate precision. Satisfied with their progress, Thomas turned his attention to the comms room, where Shade was seated, motionless, as usual.

He always seemed detached, his face impassive, like a statue carved from cold marble. His grey eyes, unnervingly snake-like, remained fixated on the enormous screen before him, which was divided into numerous smaller screens, each displaying real-time data from different locations around the globe. It was a panoramic view of the apocalypse unfolding, and Shade was the unflinching observer.

Cho was nowhere in sight, likely off inspecting the tech gear to pass the time. Thomas took a deep breath and approached Shade, his footsteps echoing slightly in the cavernous room.

"So, uh, Shade," Thomas began, his voice slightly hesitant but firm. "We, ehm, we need to get these drones and missiles connected to the control panel here. The military technicians engineered the software, but I, well, *we* need you to interface it with our system so we can steer them from this location. We also need to provide remote access to Fort Blackwood."

For a moment, there was no response. Shade remained perfectly still, his eyes fixed on the screens. The silence stretched on, making Thomas wonder if Shade had even heard him. Then, almost imperceptibly, Shade's grey eyes moved, shifting to the corner where Thomas stood. The way Shade's gaze locked onto his made Thomas' skin crawl, a primal fear creeping up his spine.

Shade's face remained expressionless, but the intensity in his eyes was palpable. Without a word, Shade extended his hand, silently asking for the drive containing the software. Thomas hesitated for a fraction of a second, then placed the small drive into Shade's open palm. The moment it touched Shade's hand, the air in the room seemed to grow colder.

Shade didn't acknowledge Thomas further. He simply turned back to the screens, plugging the drive into the console before him. His fingers moved with inhuman speed across the keyboard, a blur of motion as he began integrating the software into the bunker's systems. Code flashed across the screens, too fast for Thomas to follow, but he knew better than to question Shade's abilities.

As Shade worked, the main screen flickered, and an unofficial battle plan was received from Fort Blackwood, bearing Major General Whitmore's approval. The plan outlined a coordinated assault on the incoming threats, with the drones and missiles playing a crucial role in defending against the fire giant nearing Russia and any other entities that might emerge.

Thomas watched as the bunker's systems came to life, the drones and missiles now connected and ready for remote operation. Shade's work was flawless, as always, and Thomas couldn't help but feel a mixture of awe and unease at the efficiency with which the enigmatic figure operated.

"All set," Shade finally spoke, his voice flat and devoid of emotion. He didn't look at Thomas, his attention already shifting to the next task. "The drones and missiles are linked to the control panel. Remote access granted to Fort Blackwood."

Thomas nodded, swallowing the lump in his throat. "Good work," he managed to say, though he knew Shade didn't need the praise. "Let's hope this is enough."

Shade didn't respond. He was already moving on, his mind several steps ahead, calculating and planning for contingencies Thomas couldn't even begin to fathom.

As Thomas walked back to his station, he couldn't shake the feeling that they were all just pawns in a game far larger than any of them understood. The war against the otherworldly beings was intensifying, and the machines were ready (as ready as they could ever be), but whether they could turn the tide of this battle remained to be seen.

* * *

The mess hall's fluorescent lights cast a cold, almost sad glow over the empty tables and chairs. Nadia sat alone at one of the tables, her posture slouched and her eyes fixed on the tablet in front of her. The tray of food beside her remained untouched, forgotten in the swirl of thoughts that consumed her.

The tablet's screen showed the live feed of Casca, the elongated, eyeless entity she had been assigned to monitor. Casca was once more encased in a capsule; its unnerving form curled up in the tight space. Nadia had arranged for the creature to roam its enclosure, believing that the freedom might calm it, but her methods had been met with disapproval. And his most recent feat had cost her her digital access keys.

Her thoughts drifted, her mind grappling with the enormity of the global crisis. The reports she had overheard spoke of unimaginable horrors—mutations in the seas, tears in the skies, and monstrous beings emerging from the earth itself. She wondered about the world outside the bunker, about the fate of her family, and most painfully, about her Uncle Marcus.

Then there was Thomas. In the past two days, he had seemed to age years. The spark of excitement and curiosity that had once defined him was gone, replaced by a grim determination that was unsettling to see in someone so young. She had seen him earlier, rushing through the bunker with the cadets, overseeing the deployment of drones and missiles. He had barely glanced her way, his focus entirely on the task at hand.

As she continued to stare at the screen, lost in her thoughts, the door to the mess hall creaked open. The sound barely registered with her until she heard the soft shuffle of footsteps approaching. She didn't need to look up to know who it was. Thomas, gangly and awkward as ever, slid into the seat beside her. He didn't speak at first, simply leaned down to rest his chin on her shoulder with a sigh. His presence, as unexpected as it was, brought a small, weary smile to her lips.

"Hey," Thomas said, reaching out to pick up a carrot stick from her tray. "We've got the drones and missiles ready. They're all set to launch."

She didn't respond immediately, her eyes still fixed on the screen. "Shade?"

"Yeah," Thomas shuddered, biting into the carrot and chewing. "He handled the whole thing. Creepy as always, but... we needed him."

She nodded slightly, looking a bit amused. Shade's unnerving presence was something they had all grown accustomed to, but there was something about Thomas' reaction that made her feel a bit lighter. Even in the midst of all this, finding comfort in a friend was rare and precious.

He continued, his voice soft as he added, "There's something else, Nadia. They spotted something... a fire giant or something like it. It's heading towards Russia."

At those words, she stiffened. Her gaze finally shifted from the tablet to meet his eyes, her expression one of growing concern. "Thomas, we're in Ukraine. That thing is headed right towards us."

* * *

General Samuel Whitmore stood in the command center of Fort Blackwood, his brow furrowed with stress. The screens before him displayed live feeds from the front lines, satellite images, and an array of tactical maps detailing the global situation. Despite the chaos, his focus was on a single task: making contact with the Russian military.

The room buzzed with activity, soldiers, and officers moving about with purpose, their faces set in determination. Whitmore took a deep breath, mentally preparing himself for the call he was about to make. He knew this would be no easy task. The U.S. and Russia had a long history of rivalry—geopolitical, ideological, and economic tensions that had only grown over the years. But now, they faced a common enemy, one that threatened the very existence of humanity. He had to make them see that...once he fully accepted it as well.

Whitmore's comms officer, Captain Jackson, looked up from his station, nodding to the general. "Sir, the secure line to the Russian command is open. They're waiting for you."

Whitmore gave a curt nod and stepped forward. He pressed a button on the console, and the call connected. The crackle of static cleared, revealing the stern voice of a Russian officer on the other end.

"General Whitmore," the translator's voice came through, translating the Russian's words into English with precise, almost clinical accuracy. "This is Colonel Keehl of the Russian Armed Forces. To what do we owe this...unexpected communication?"

Whitmore could hear the underlying suspicion in Keehl's tone, the barely concealed distrust. He cleared his throat, keeping his own voice steady and authoritative. "Colonel Keehl, we're facing a mutual threat. A fire giant—a creature of immense power—is moving towards your shores. It's currently in the waters off the coast of Ukraine, not far from your western borders."

There was a brief pause, filled only with the distant hum of machinery. "We are aware of it," his words were laced with skepticism. "And what do you propose, General? A joint operation? We've heard this kind of talk before, only to find ourselves on the receiving end of your nation's so-called 'assistance.'"

Whitmore clenched his jaw. He knew the Russian perspective all too well—decades of distrust had built a wall between their nations, and breaking through it now, in the midst of a global crisis, was going to be a challenge.

"We have actionable intel," Whitmore pressed on. "Our drones and missile systems are ready to engage, but we need to coordinate our efforts. If this creature reaches the shore, it will be catastrophic for both of our countries. We can't afford to let politics get in the way of survival."

The translator's voice relayed his message to Keehl, and another pause followed. Whitmore could almost picture the Russian colonel on the other end, weighing his options and considering the risks.

"Why should we trust you, General?" Keehl's voice came through, cold and calculating. "Your forces have always been more concerned with your own interests than with true cooperation. How do we know this isn't another ploy?"

Before Whitmore could respond, another voice cut in—Marcus Flynn, his Irish accent seeping through in his moment of frustration. "Christ Almighty, the pair o' yous, we haven't got time fer dis! That bloody giant's closer to yer shores than it is to our bunker in Ukraine. If it makes landfall, none of us are safe, ya bollocks!"

Whitmore shot Marcus a sharp look, but he didn't interrupt. Marcus was right, and the urgency in his voice was palpable. This wasn't just about national pride or political games—it was about survival.

The Russian colonel's response was slow, deliberate. "That is…well, it is correct. The creature is closer to our territory. But understand this, General: if we agree to cooperate, we do so on equal terms. No more of your country's high-handed tactics. We share information, we coordinate our strikes, and we ensure the safety of our people. Do we have an agreement?"

Whitmore exhaled, the tension in his chest easing slightly. It wasn't perfect, but it was a start. "Agreed, Colonel Keehl. We'll send over our latest intel on the creature's position and movements. Let's keep this line open—our forces need to be in constant communication."

The translator relayed his words, and after a moment, Keehl responded. "Understood. We'll mobilize our forces and prepare for joint action. But mark my words, General: this is a temporary alliance. Once this threat is neutralized, we go back to business as usual."

"Fair enough," Whitmore replied, his tone measured. "But let's make sure there's still a world left to argue over."

The line went dead, and Whitmore turned to his team, his expression hardening. "Jackson, get the intel packet ready and send it over to the Russians. I want real-time updates on the creature's movements and to make sure our drones are prepped for launch. We're going to hit this thing with everything we've got."

As the room erupted into action, Marcus stepped closer, his voice low. "You think they'll play ball, General?"

Whitmore glanced at him, his gaze steely. "They don't have a choice, Marcus. None of us do."

Marcus nodded, though his face remained tight with concern. He turned to pet Max, who was lazing in a corner of the room, then looked back at Whitmore. "We're all in this together, whether we like it or not."

"Damn right," Whitmore muttered, his eyes narrowing as he watched the flurry of activity around him. "Now, let's make sure we're the ones left standing when this is over."

* * *

Hours later, the command center was a hub of frenetic energy as the exchange of intel between the U.S. and Russian forces progressed. The massive screens along the walls displayed real-time satellite imagery and data streams, detailing the movements of the titan as it trudged through the frigid waters off the coast of Ukraine, heading toward Russia. The creature's every step was monitored closely, and the reports were grim.

General Whitmore stood at the center of the room, arms crossed, his face a mask of grim determination. Around him, officers barked orders, relayed information, and coordinated the next steps. He watched the live feed, the colossal figure of the titan moving with an unsettling, relentless purpose. The water around it steamed and crackled as the ice formed and broke under the heat radiating from its body.

A junior officer approached, handing Whitmore a report. "General, the Russians have confirmed their drones are picking up the same observations. They're deploying additional forces to the coastline, but they're still figuring out how to best contain it. The cold's working, but it's not enough."

Whitmore nodded, his mind racing through the possibilities. "Have we considered using the environment to our advantage? If we could trap it in deeper waters or lure it into a position where it's more vulnerable…"

"We're looking into it, sir," the officer replied. "But with the size of this thing… we'd need more than just cold water. Maybe some sort of containment or coordinated strike once it's further immobilized."

As Whitmore processed this, the door to the command center opened, and the surviving team led by John Harrows entered, looking every bit as battered as the reports coming in. Their armor was scratched, scorched, and, in some cases, barely holding together, but they were alive. That was more than could be said for many others.

Harrows, still in his damaged suit, moved directly toward the main screens, his gaze fixed on the images of the titan. He ignored the officers who approached to check on him, waving them off as he tried to absorb the situation. His mind was still reeling from the chaos they had left behind in Switzerland, but there was no time for rest. Max, his loyal dog, bolted from where he had been lying down and leaped up to greet him. Harrows gave the dog a rough pat, his mind already back in the fight. The sounds of the command center buzzed around him, but his focus was on the figure of the titan slowly advancing through the dark waters.

"Sir, you need to let us treat those wounds," one of the medics insisted, approaching with a first aid kit.

"Not now," Harrows grunted, his eyes never leaving the screen. "I'm not leaving this fight. What's our status?"

Whitmore stepped forward, handing him a report. "The titan's movement is slower than we anticipated, thanks to the cold, but it's still coming. My men estimate it'll reach the shore in seven to eight hours. The Russians are deploying forces, but we need to come up with a way to take this thing down before it gets to land."

Harrows scanned the report, his expression darkening. "We need something more… something that can either trap it or break it down."

As they spoke, more suits were being crafted in the team's absence. Engineers and technicians worked tirelessly in another section of the fort, assembling the advanced armor for the next battalion and preparing to intervene. The suits had been improved, incorporating the lessons learned from the battle in Switzerland. Reinforced plating, enhanced cooling systems, and better protection against both extreme heat and cold were integrated, making them more resilient against the elemental forces they were up against.

Harrows noticed the preparations on the screen and nodded in approval. "We'll need every advantage we can get. But if we're going to make a real difference, we need to hit it hard. Have the drones and missiles been prepped?"

"Thomas and Shade are working on it," Whitmore replied. "They've connected the control panels, and we're coordinating with the Russians to ensure a synchronized strike. But we need to figure out where to hit it and how."

An hour passed as the teams on both sides scrambled to come up with a viable strategy. The fort's command center was a hive of activity, with calls being made, data analyzed, and battle plans formulated. Harrows stayed in the thick of it, contributing where he could, his mind sharp despite the exhaustion weighing down his body.

Finally, Thomas's voice came through the comms, breaking the tense silence. "General Whitmore, Mr. Harrows… we've got something. Satellite imagery and thermal scans show a vulnerability in the titan's structure. Its legs are under the most stress from the cold. If we can focus our attacks there, we might be able to bring it down — or at least slow it enough to contain it."

Whitmore leaned forward, his eyes narrowing as he studied the data being displayed on the screen. "What do you suggest?"

Thomas hesitated for a moment before continuing. "We use the drones to target the weakest points with concentrated missile strikes. Simultaneously, we deploy teams to the shore to engage and distract it, drawing its attention away from the drones. The Russians have agreed to assist with heavy artillery and air support. It's a long shot, but it's our best option."

Harrows nodded. "It's risky, but it might work. We don't have time for anything else."

Whitmore straightened, his voice commanding as he began to issue orders. "Alright, let's get those drones in position. Prepare the teams for deployment. We hit that thing with everything we've got and pray it's enough."

The room erupted into motion once more as the final preparations were made. Harrows, his mind already in the battle ahead, glanced down at Max, who sat patiently by his side. He gave the dog a brief, reassuring pat before turning back to the screen, his expression hard as steel.

* * *

The sky above the Barents Sea was a vast expanse of cobalt blue, the sun just beginning to dip below the horizon. Below, the icy waters moved to their own tune. However, the peacefulness of the scene was shattered by the immense form of the titan, a hulking mass of molten rock and fire, trudging relentlessly toward the coastline.

High above, the U.S. battalion, clad in their cutting-edge nano-technological armor, soared through the air. The suits, a marvel of modern engineering, were sleek and adaptive, their dark surfaces reflecting the faint light of the moon. Built-in hover systems in the soles of their boots allowed the soldiers to maneuver effortlessly across the sky while the advanced exoskeletons enhanced their strength and agility. Each soldier carried laser weapons and specialized ammunition—highly dangerous, armor-piercing rounds designed to penetrate the titan's dense exterior.

As they descended toward the titan, the soldiers spread out in a strategic formation. Their HUDs flickered with real-time data, showing weak points in the titan's structure as identified by the drone reconnaissance earlier. The air was filled with the hum of energy weapons powering up and the sharp crackle of comms as they coordinated their assault.

"Focus on the legs!" their commanding officer, Major Grant, barked over the comms. "We need to slow it down before it reaches the shore. Keep your distance, and don't get caught in its line of fire!"

The titan below was a terrifying sight. Each of its steps caused the ground beneath the ocean to tremble, sending massive waves crashing in every direction. The ice forming around its legs barely seemed to impede its progress. As the soldiers unleashed their initial volley, beams of concentrated laser fire and bursts of high-velocity rounds streaked through the air, slamming into the titan's legs. Explosions of molten rock and steam erupted from the impact point, but the titan barely slowed.

Suddenly, the titan's head tilted upward as if sensing the assault from above. Its massive, molten hand swung through the air, trying to swat the soldiers away like gnats. The heat radiating from its body intensified, and the air around it shimmered with the rising temperature. One of the soldiers veered too close, and the titan's hand came down in a fiery arc, threatening to incinerate him on the spot.

Major Grant's heart lurched as he watched the scene unfold in his HUD. The soldier was about to be obliterated—until a streak of white flashed across his vision.

A bright white-armored individual, moving with impossible speed, fired a precision shot that struck the titan's hand. The impact was powerful enough to deflect the titan's blow, saving the soldier from certain death. Major Grant's eyes widened as he scanned the sky, searching for the source of the shot.

More white-armored figures appeared, cutting through the sky with a grace and precision that matched the U.S. soldiers. Their armor was different—sleeker, more angular, and unmistakably Russian. The symbols on their chests were a mix of old Soviet designs and modern Russian military insignia. They moved in tight formations, their weapons crackling with energy as they joined the fray.

A sudden beep in Major Grant's HUD alerted him to an incoming audio signal. He hesitated for a moment before accepting it, and the voice of a woman, cool and authoritative, came through his earpiece.

"Lieutenant Plisetskaya of the Russian Armed Forces," she introduced herself. "We are ready to proceed with the plan. Your men are holding up well, Major."

Major Grant quickly surveyed the situation, assessing the new arrivals. The Russians were here, and they were prepared. He nodded to himself, his respect for his newfound allies growing. "Good to have you with us, Lieutenant. Let's bring this bastard down."

The Russian forces seamlessly integrated into the U.S. battalion's formation, their white armor glowing faintly against the twilight sky. The combined might of both armies now bore down on the titan, their synchronized attacks hitting its legs with relentless force. The titan roared, a deep, guttural sound that shook the very air around them, but the combined firepower was taking its toll.

As the battle raged on, the U.S. and Russian forces coordinated their movements with surgical precision. The sky was alight with bursts of energy and the streaks of tracer rounds. Below, the titan's progress was finally slowing, its massive legs struggling against the ice and the barrage of attacks.

The soldiers, both American and Russian, pressed on with renewed determination, knowing that their combined efforts were the only thing standing between the titan and the destruction of everything in its path.

Chapter 8: Call of the Horizon

The sky was a warzone.

Both Russian and American soldiers darted through the air, their advanced nano-tech suits thrumming with energy as they executed maneuvers that would have been impossible just years ago. Each suit was a masterpiece of engineering, equipped with built-in hover systems, integrated tactical displays, and adaptive armor that could withstand heat, pressure, and even some of the titan's brutal strikes—though not always for long. Below them, the titan continued its mindless march, molten rock dripping from its colossal body and hissing as it made contact with the icy waters of the Barents Sea.

The soldiers strafed the giant, their laser rifles flashing with bursts of concentrated energy. They aimed for the weak points that had been mapped out by their drones, though landing a shot on a moving target of such size and strength was easier said than done. With every step the titan took, waves crashed violently against its legs while great plumes of steam rose where fire met ice. The titan's molten hand swung again, and this time, one of the Russian soldiers wasn't quick enough.

The soldier—a Captain by the markings on his white armor— was swatted out of the air like a fly. The titan's fiery palm struck him hard, sending him tumbling in a smoking arc before he plunged into the cold sea below. His suit's emergency cooling systems had activated too late, and the searing heat had burned through portions of the armor, exposing charred flesh. The man splashed into the water, lifeless.

"Damn it!" Major Grant hissed through his teeth as he narrowly dodged another swipe of the titan's hand. "Everyone, stay sharp! Don't get too close!"

But the titan was unstoppable. Its movements were slow but powerful, and even with its feet encased in ice, it continued to fight back. Several more soldiers found themselves dodging molten debris, chunks of burning rock raining down from the titan's body as their weapons struck home. One of the Americans managed to land a well-placed shot on the titan's shoulder, blowing off a slab of fiery stone, but the resulting explosion sent him spiraling out of control.

"Get him out of there!" Grant shouted, but before anyone could respond, the Russian soldier was gone—swallowed by the icy sea below, his body still ablaze.

Grant gritted his teeth, focusing all his energy on the task at hand. The titan's right hand was moving to swat another group of soldiers out of the sky, and he lined up his shot. His laser rifle hummed as it charged, then released a searing beam of energy straight into the titan's hand. The result was immediate—three of the titan's massive fingers exploded into fiery fragments, spraying molten debris across the sky.

"I need something strong to forget this," Grant muttered to himself as he pulled back to reassess.

But before he could catch his breath, the titan's remaining hand swung toward one of the Russian soldiers who had been hovering dangerously close. The soldier, Lieutenant Agapov, didn't see it coming—his attention was on stabilizing himself after the last wave of attacks.

Without hesitation, one of Grant's men, Sergeant Rodriguez, dove between Agapov and the titan's flailing hand. He fired a short burst from his thrusters, propelling himself just fast enough to tackle Agapov out of the way. The titan's hand missed them by inches, but the sheer heat radiating from it scorched the armor on Rodriguez's back, melting part of his suit.

Rodriguez and Agapov hit the cold sea hard, their bodies disappearing beneath the surface. For a moment, Grant thought they were gone too, but after a few tense seconds, both soldiers reemerged from the water. Agapov's white armor was battered but intact, while Rodriguez's suit was sizzling, patches of melted metal cooling in the frigid water.

"Rodriguez, report!" Grant barked into the comms, his voice tight with concern.

"Alive, sir," Rodriguez coughed, his voice strained but steady. "Just... a little toasted."

Grant felt a brief surge of relief but quickly refocused. The battle was far from over, and every second they delayed brought the Titan closer to land. Despite their best efforts, the creature was still standing, still moving forward. Even with three of its fingers, part of its right shoulder blown off, the titan continued to lash out, each swing of its remaining hand a deadly threat to anyone who got too close.

Above them, more soldiers circled, their laser weapons and specialized rounds hammering away at the Titan. Some soldiers had switched tactics, using the environment to their advantage—firing nitrogen rays into the waters surrounding the Titan's feet to create more ice, hoping to slow it down even further. Others attempted to target its head, though the heat radiating from the titan's core made it nearly impossible to approach without risking their suits overheating.

A squad of Russian soldiers coordinated an aerial assault, launching synchronized missiles at the Titan's chest. The impact was thunderous, sending shockwaves through the air and causing the Titan to stumble slightly. For a moment, it looked like the combined assault was working.

But then the Titan let out a deafening roar, a sound that shook the very heavens. It raised its remaining hand and slammed it into the sea with immense force, sending up a tidal wave of freezing water and molten rock. Several soldiers were caught in the blast, their suits barely holding together as they were hurled through the air like rag dolls.

"We're not out of this yet!" Grant yelled, scanning the battlefield. He could see that the Titan was slowing—its legs encased in more and more ice with every step—but it wasn't enough. They needed to find a way to topple the Titan entirely, to bring it down before it reached the shore.

"Keep up the pressure!" he ordered. "We take this thing down, or it's over for all of us!"

As the soldiers redoubled their efforts, the skies over the Barents Sea remained a chaotic storm of fire and ice, and the fight to stop the Titan raged on.

The battlefield in the skies above the Barents Sea was unforgiving. Despite their advanced armor and weapons, the soldiers were dropping one by one, the Titan's relentless assault proving to be too much for some. Major Grant, hovering above the chaos, took a brief moment to assess the situation. The toll was staggering. His HUD displayed the dwindling number of active soldiers, each one a reminder of the men and women he had lost.

With a deep breath, Grant opened a secure channel to Fort Blackwood.

"Control, this is Major Grant. We're down by too many men—requesting immediate support or fallback orders," he reported, his voice steady but laced with the strain of battle. He could hear the static crackle in his earpiece as the transmission was relayed back to command.

Inside Fort Blackwood, Harrows listened intently to Grant's report. They were losing ground, and despite the technology and the training, the Titan's sheer size and power were proving to be nearly insurmountable. Harrows clenched his fists, knowing what needed to be done.

"Jack, don't even think about it," Whitmore's voice cut through the comms as he noticed Harrows pulling on his nano-tech suit. But Harrows, with a determined set to his jaw, didn't stop.

"I'm going, Sam," Harrows said firmly, his voice leaving no room for argument. "Those are my men out there, and I'm not going to sit back while they get torn apart. We need every hand on deck, and I'm not staying here while they fight for their lives."

"You're more valuable here. You know that," Whitmore countered, though his tone lacked the bite it usually had. Even he knew that the situation was dire.

Harrows paused, his suit zipped halfway up. He turned to face Whitmore, his eyes burning with the kind of resolve that only years of leadership could forge. "We're beyond value now, Sam. We're at survival. If we don't stop that thing, there won't be a Fort Blackwood left to command."

Whitmore stared at him, the weight of the words settling into his bones. But before he could respond, another transmission came through, this time from the Ukrainian bunker.

"This is Cadet Lee at the Ukrainian bunker," a young, slightly panicked voice came through the comms. "We've been feeling minor earthquakes for the past hour. They're getting stronger. If this continues... we might have to consider evacuation. Is surface access an option?"

Harrows exchanged a quick glance with Whitmore. The situation was escalating on all fronts. The thought of those stationed in the bunker having to evacuate in the midst of everything else was another layer of complication they didn't need. But he knew they couldn't ignore the risk.

"Son, this is Harrows," he responded, keeping his voice as calm as possible. "We're monitoring the situation. For now, hold your position. If those quakes get any worse, we'll assess the risk of evacuation. But understand, getting to the surface isn't a guarantee of safety. We'll be in touch."

The line went silent for a moment, only the distant sounds of hushed whispers and the tremors echoing through the background.

Lee's voice came back, a bit steadier. "Understood, sir. We'll hold until further orders."

As the connection closed, Harrows finished pulling on his suit, the sleek black material sealing around him with a hiss. He activated the suit's systems, feeling the surge of power as the HUD came to life in front of his eyes. He was ready.

Whitmore watched him for a moment longer, then sighed heavily. "You better make it back, Jack."

"Don't worry," Harrows replied with a slight grin, though it didn't reach his eyes. "I'm too stubborn to die out there."

With that, Harrows headed toward the exit. Max, his devoted dog, barked and trotted alongside him, sensing the fear in his master's demeanor. Harrows gave him a pat on the head as they reached the launch bay, and Max, understanding, stayed behind.

As Harrows prepared to join the fight in the Barents Sea, the situation continued to deteriorate. The Titan's march was relentless, and despite their best efforts, the soldiers were struggling to find a way to bring it down. Harrows knew that when he arrived, he would be entering a battle that could very well be his last.

But that didn't matter. What mattered was the mission and the lives depending on it.

With a final glance back at Fort Blackwood, Harrows stepped into the launch bay, ready to face whatever awaited him in the icy skies above.

The cold wind swept across the New Dawn facility. Its once bustling energy was now replaced by an unnerving calm as the last of the trucks rumbled away, disappearing into the horizon. Dr. Evelyn Shaw stood at the edge of the loading bay, tugging her warm shawl tighter around her shoulders. The fabric was a small comfort against the chill that seemed to seep into her bones. The trucks carried the disassembled parts of the Large Hadron Collider, a project she had once held with such pride and ambition, now reduced to pieces being transported for a purpose far grimmer than she had ever imagined.

Her gaze shifted to the final truck in the convoy, where Leo, the driver, and Debbie, an engineer, were suited up in their protective HAZMAT suits. This particular truck carried the most dangerous cargo of all—the encapsulated energy core that had powered the entire machine. Its ominous presence was a reminder of the power they had tampered with, a power they were now desperate to contain.

As the truck disappeared from view, Evelyn's eyes settled on Jeremiah, standing a few feet away, watching the convoy leave with a stoic expression. He was tall, his broad shoulders slightly hunched as if the weight of the world rested upon them. His weathered face, framed by greying hair that had once been a deep brown, showed the signs of age and countless sleepless nights. His eyes, a piercing blue, held a depth of knowledge and pain that only someone who had seen too much could carry. The lines on his face spoke of a life lived in the trenches of scientific discovery, where the price of progress often came at a personal cost.

Jeremiah didn't turn to look at her, but Evelyn knew he was aware of her stare. She could sense the tension in the air, an unresolved past that lingered between them. After a long moment, he sighed deeply, the sound heavy with resignation.

"I helped because it's the fate of humanity at stake," he said, his voice low yet firm. "And because… because I couldn't bear to see you distressed or physically hurt when you called about the…whatever on God's green earth that was."

His words, though sincere, were tinged with a harshness that cut deep. Evelyn could hear the pain buried beneath his calm exterior, even if he tried to hide it. His face remained set, the muscles in his jaw tightening as if to keep any trace of emotion from showing. But his eyes—those eyes that had seen so much—couldn't completely mask the hurt.

"But know this," he continued, still not meeting her gaze. "It doesn't change anything between us. Not after what happened last time."

Evelyn nodded slowly, accepting his words for what they were— a boundary that he was unwilling to cross again. The memory of their last fallout still haunted them both, a scar that had never fully healed.

"I understand," she said softly, her voice carrying a note of regret. The wind picked up again, and she pulled her shawl closer, the chill now feeling less like the weather and more like the cold distance between them. "I just wanted to ask… Are you still using the accommodations within the facility? Like most of the out-of-state employees?"

Jeremiah grunted in response, a noncommittal sound that could have meant anything, but Evelyn knew him well enough to interpret it as a yes.

She hesitated for a moment before speaking again, her concern for him overriding the tension between them. "It's not safe here anymore, Jeremiah. The whole place has been evacuated now. You're welcome to come to my place instead… unless you already have other arrangements."

Her offer hung in the air between them, a tentative olive branch that she wasn't sure he would accept. Jeremiah finally turned to face her, his eyes meeting hers with a mixture of surprise and something else she couldn't quite place.

For a brief moment, the old connection they once shared flickered in his gaze, but it was quickly extinguished as he closed himself off again, his expression unreadable.

"I'll think about it," he replied, his voice devoid of the warmth that had once been there. He gave her a small, barely noticeable nod before turning away, his broad back once again facing her as he walked toward the facility's main entrance.

Evelyn watched him go, her heart heavy with the knowledge that the chasm between them was still wide and deep. Yet, she couldn't help but hope that maybe, just maybe, they could find a way to bridge it, even if only for a little while longer.

As the night skies watched over her, she turned and headed to her car. The sound of the trucks' engines was still echoing in her mind. There was so much at stake, so much more to be done, but in that moment, all she could think about was the man who had once been her closest ally—and the distance that now separated them.

* * *

The underground bunker in Ukraine was a fortress of steel and concrete, designed to withstand almost anything the world—or other worlds—could throw at it. But even here, deep beneath the earth, the tremors were felt. Minor earthquakes shook the walls, causing dust to trickle down from the ceiling and sending waves of unease through the civilian specialists and military personnel stationed there. The tension in the air was palpable, each quake a reminder of the unstable reality they were now living in.

In the dimly lit control room, a group of young cadets, seasoned officers, and even cyber terrorists like Shade and Cho monitored the situation closely. Screens flickered with data, surveillance feeds, and tactical overlays. However, the primary focus was on the containment units where the entities were held. These were no ordinary creatures—they were beings from another dimension, each more dangerous and unpredictable than the last.

The engineers had made the containment capsules even more secure, reinforcing them with additional layers of protection, especially for the most volatile of the entities—Pink Eye. The creature, a nightmarish mass of shifting, parasitic eyes, had earned its name from the way it infected anything it touched, spreading like a disease. Nadia Ayoub, whose access had been revoked due to her more empathetic approach to dealing with one of these beings, had nonetheless suggested that they annihilate the entities out of caution. The room had fallen silent at her suggestion. It was entirely opposite from her previous stance, and it underscored the seriousness of the situation.

"We've gathered enough data," Nadia had argued. "We can't risk any of them getting out. Pink Eye needs to be destroyed."

There was a murmur of agreement, but when she proposed sparing one entity—Casca—the room grew tense again.

"Casca isn't like the others," she explained. "He's more predictable, more... trainable, in a way. If we keep him, we might learn something that could help us in the long run. His weaknesses are as normal as any animal's or human's. We can control him."

The suggestion was met with skepticism but not outright rejection. After some deliberation, it was agreed that Casca would be spared for now. The decision was a calculated risk, but in a world gone mad, it was one they were willing to take.

While the cadets moved to destroy the other entities, Nadia found herself standing beside the seat of a young comms officer. He was fresh-faced, likely in his early twenties, with a look of determination that belied his youth. The screen in front of him displayed the live feed from the lab where the entities were being euthanized. Her presence beside him seemed to make the young man slightly nervous, his cheeks flushing as she leaned over his shoulder to point something out on the screen.

"There," she said, her voice calm but urgent. "In the corner. Part of the symbiote managed to escape the torching."

The officer's eyes widened as he spotted the writhing mass, a part of the creature that had slipped away from the flames. He quickly keyed in the microphone, his voice steady despite the tension.

"Team, you've got a piece of the entity in the southeast corner. Use the flamethrower on it immediately."

There was a moment of panic visible on the screen as the lab team, clad in their heavily protective HAZMAT suits, scrambled to locate and neutralize the rogue piece of the creature. The goop slithered across the floor, its slimy mass already searching for a host. But the soldiers acted swiftly, one of them dousing it in a torrent of fire, incinerating it completely.

The screen displayed the charred remains, now inert and harmless. The officer sighed in relief, his fingers still hovering over the controls as the room settled back into a tense silence.

Nadia remained beside him, her eyes fixed on the screen. She could feel the fear and anxiety radiating from those around her, but she kept her composure. Her mind was a whirlwind of thoughts—about the global crisis, the uncertainty of their situation, the people currently around her, her family, Thomas, who had been keeping everything in check, and most of all, her Uncle Marcus.

Both Nadia and Thomas had been placed in roles where they had to acutely fit into the shoes of their superiors despite being at the grassroots levels compared to them in terms of both their age and professional experience.

The officer beside her glanced up, giving her an awkward, lopsided smile as he met her gaze. Nadia blinked for a second before averting her eyes as a gentle pink dusted her otherwise dusky cheeks. She cleared her throat, thanking him and appreciating his diligence in such a high-stakes environment. The officer's smile widened as he turned his attention back to his screen, a bit of his confidence restored by genuine appreciation and acknowledgment.

The bunker might have been shaking and the world outside might have been in chaos, however, for now, they had done what needed to be done. The symbiote was no more, and the threat had been contained. But as Nadia looked at the containment unit holding Casca, she knew that their challenges were far from over.

* * *

The arctic winds howled through the skies over the Barents Sea, swirling around the soldiers who hovered mid-air in their advanced nano-technological suits. The bleak, icy expanse below was only interrupted by the enormous figure of the Titan, a massive, fiery behemoth that lumbered towards the Russian coastline with terrifying purpose. The creature's molten skin glowed against the cold backdrop, steam hissing where its feet touched the frozen waters, causing the ice to crack and melt beneath it. Each of its steps sent shockwaves through the earth, echoing across the desolate sea.

Major Grant and Lieutenant Plisetskaya, both seasoned and battle-hardened, led their respective teams—American and Russian soldiers—into the fray, their HUDs (Heads-Up Displays) synchronized for a joint offensive. Despite years of geopolitical tensions and mistrust between their nations, necessity had forged a temporary alliance in the face of a threat that neither side could afford to ignore. The Titan had to be stopped, and they were the only ones standing between it and untold destruction.

"Major Grant, I've received new orders from the Russian control tower," Lieutenant Plisetskaya's voice crackled over the comms. Her tone was steady, her accent thick, but her English clear. "We need to focus our fire on the Titan's knee joints and lower legs. If we can destabilize it, we might be able to slow it down."

"Copy that, Lieutenant," Grant responded, his voice gruff and laced with determination. "Relay the formation to your team. We'll synchronize our assault."

Plisetskaya nodded, even though he couldn't see her. "Understood. Team, fall into offensive formation Delta-5. Focus fire on the target's lower extremities."

The Russian soldiers acknowledged the command, their responses clipped and efficient. In a coordinated maneuver, they shifted into position, forming a semi-circle around the Titan's legs. The Americans did the same, their movements synchronized with their Russian counterparts. The two forces, once adversaries, now worked as a single unit, their combined firepower aimed at the creature's vulnerable points.

"Steady, men… fire!" Major Grant's order was met with a volley of projectiles, laser beams, and high-explosive rounds that rained down on the Titan's knees and ankles. The air was filled with the whir of advanced weaponry, the soldiers' suits humming as they discharged their payloads. Red beams from laser rifles cut through the cold, slamming into the creature's joints, while concussive rounds exploded against its hardened skin.

The Titan roared in fury, its voice a deafening rumble that shook the sky. It staggered slightly, its massive legs trembling under the concentrated fire. But it wasn't enough to bring it down. The creature's molten form seemed almost impervious to their attacks, the flames on its body intensifying as it swung its enormous arms at the soldiers buzzing around it like gnats.

"Watch out!" Plisetskaya shouted as the Titan's hand came crashing down, trying to swat them out of the air. The soldiers scattered, using the hover systems in their suits to dart away from the massive fist. One of the Russian soldiers wasn't quick enough—he was caught in the Titan's swipe and sent hurtling into the icy waters below, his suit's emergency systems struggling to keep him afloat.

"We're not doing enough damage!" One of the American soldiers, Sergeant Blake, called out over the comms, frustration evident in his voice. "This thing's still moving towards the coast!"

"Keep firing! Focus on the knees!" Major Grant barked back, his voice cutting through the chaos. "We've got to slow it down!"

The soldiers redoubled their efforts, their weapons heating up as they unleashed another barrage of firepower. Explosions rippled across the Titan's legs and for a moment, it seemed like they were making progress. The creature stumbled, its forward momentum slowing as it fought to maintain its balance.

But the Titan was far from defeated. With a screech that made the very air tremble, it lashed out again, its fiery hand sweeping across the sky. Two more soldiers were caught in the swing, their suits barely protecting them from the heat as they were flung into the sea. The icy water hissed and boiled where the Titan's flames touched, sending up clouds of steam that obscured the battlefield.

"Stay focused!" Plisetskaya ordered; her voice sharp with urgency. "We're not done yet!"

Just as the Titan raised its foot to crush one of the soldiers below, a new voice crackled over the comms. "Harrows here, deploying now. I'm joining the fight."

Major Grant's eyes widened behind his visor as he watched Harrows soar into view, his suit gleaming under the pale rising Arctic sun. Harrows had been deployed via the launch pad, and his arrival couldn't have been more perfectly timed. With a quick adjustment of his HUD, Grant linked up with Harrows' comms just as the man unleashed a torrent of fire on the Titan.

"Glad you could make it," Grant said, his voice tinged with relief. "We could use the firepower."

Harrows didn't respond verbally, but his actions spoke louder than words. He fired a concentrated burst from a liquid nitrogen blaster, aiming directly at the Titan's chest. The blast hit its mark, the intense cold clashing with the creature's fiery core. Steam erupted from the point of impact and for the first time, the Titan's advance faltered. It toppled slightly, struggling to regain its balance as the cold spread across its chest, hardening the molten rock into brittle stone.

"Now!" Plisetskaya shouted. "Hit the legs, now!"

The soldiers didn't hesitate. They fired everything they had, targeting the Titan's already weakened knees and ankles. Explosions rippled across its joints, the combined firepower of both the American and Russian forces finally taking its toll. The Titan stumbled, its massive form swaying as it fought to stay upright.

Harrows swooped in again, this time focusing on the creature's other leg. Another burst of liquid nitrogen struck home, freezing the Titan's ankle and causing it to crack under the pressure. The creature let out a pained roar, its movements growing more sluggish as it tried to shake off the effects of the freezing blasts.

"Keep at it!" Grant urged, his voice carrying over the comms. "We've got it on the ropes!"

The soldiers pressed their attack, their suits buzzing with energy as they unleashed everything they had. More laser beams cut through the air, striking the Titan's legs with pinpoint accuracy. The creature's movements grew more erratic, its arms flailing as it tried to ward off the relentless assault.

But the Titan wasn't done yet. With a final, desperate swing, it lashed out at the soldiers hovering around its chest. The attack caught one of the Russian soldiers off guard, sending her tumbling through the air. Before she could recover, the Titan's hand was upon her, flames licking at her suit as it closed in for the kill.

"No!" Plisetskaya shouted, her voice filled with desperation.

But before the Titan could crush the soldier, Harrows swooped in once again, his liquid nitrogen blaster firing a concentrated stream at the creature's hand. The sudden cold caused the Titan's fingers to seize up and the soldier managed to escape its grasp, narrowly avoiding a fiery death.

"Thanks," the Russian soldier gasped, her voice shaky with relief.

"Don't mention it," Harrows replied, his voice calm despite the chaos around him. "Let's finish this."

The battle raged on, the soldiers continuing their assault on the Titan's legs. Major Grant took aim with his own weapon, a high-powered laser rifle, and fired a burst at the creature's knee joint. The beam sliced through the weakened rock, and with a thunderous crack, the Titan's knee gave way.

The creature screamed in pain as it staggered, its massive form lurching forward. But even as it fell, it wasn't done fighting. With a final, desperate effort, it swung its arm at the soldiers one last time, trying to take as many of them down with it as possible.

Grant saw the attack coming and reacted instinctively. He fired another burst from his laser rifle, this time targeting the Titan's already damaged hand. The beam struck true, blowing the hand clean off. The Titan howled in agony, its swing faltering as it clutched at its injured hand.

But even with its hand crippled, the Titan's momentum carried it forward, its massive form crashing towards the soldiers below. One of the Russian soldiers, still recovering from the earlier attack, was directly in its path.

"Look out!" Grant shouted, but he knew the warning wouldn't be enough. The soldier was too slow, too disoriented to dodge in time.

Without thinking, Grant dove towards the soldier, his suit's hover systems straining to keep up with the sudden acceleration. He grabbed the soldier by the arm and yanked him out of the way just as the Titan's hand came crashing down. The ground where the soldier had been standing exploded in a shower of debris, but they were safe.

"Got you," Grant said, panting slightly as he helped the soldier regain his balance.

The Russian soldier nodded; his gratitude clear in his eyes. "Thank you, Major."

"Don't mention it," Grant replied, his voice firm. "We're all in this together."

The Titan's form continued to sway, its legs buckling under the combined assault. But even as it teetered on the brink of collapse, it remained a formidable foe. Its molten skin still glowed with heat, and its eyes, burning with rage, focused on the soldiers swarming around it.

"We need to hit it harder!" Plisetskaya called out; her voice filled with determination. "Everyone, target the legs with everything you've got! We have to bring it down!"

The soldiers responded with a final, concentrated assault. Missiles streaked through the air, their trails of smoke cutting through the sky as they slammed into the Titan's legs. The explosions rocked the creature, causing the ice beneath it to crack and shatter. The Titan's balance wavered, and for a moment, it looked like it would finally topple.

But then, the Titan planted its massive hand on the ground, steadying itself. The soldiers redoubled their efforts, their weapons blazing as they fired at the Titan's hand, trying to force it to let go.

Harrows, seeing the opportunity, swooped in for a final attack. His suit's thrusters roared as he charged towards the Titan's chest, his liquid nitrogen blaster at the ready. With a precise shot, he fired directly at the creature's core, aiming for the spot where the cold had already weakened its fiery heart.

The blast struck true, and for a moment, everything seemed to freeze. The Titan's movements slowed, its molten skin hardening as the cold spread through its body. The creature let out a final, anguished roar as it struggled to fight off the effects of the freezing blast.

And then, with a sound like shattering glass, the Titan's chest cracked open. The cold had reached its core, and the creature's molten heart, once a blazing inferno, was now nothing more than a brittle, frozen shell. The Titan's body wavered, its massive form swaying as it fought to remain standing.

"Now, everyone, hit it with everything you've got!" Major Grant shouted, his voice ringing out over the comms.

The soldiers fired their final volleys, missiles, and laser beams streaking through the air as they converged on the Titan's weakened form. The explosions rocked the creature, and for a moment, it looked like it would finally fall.

But even as the Titan's legs buckled, it remained defiant. With a final, desperate effort, it raised its arm, ready to strike down one last time.

Grant and Plisetskaya both saw the attack coming, their HUDs lighting up with warnings. But there was no time to evade, no time to get out of the way. The Titan's arm was already coming down, and there was nothing they could do to stop it. But Harrows wasn't ready to give up. He swooped in one last time, his suit's thrusters roaring as he charged towards the Titan's arm. With a final burst of speed, he fired his liquid nitrogen blaster at the creature's elbow, aiming for the spot where the joint was already weakened.

The blast hit home, freezing the Titan's arm in mid-swing. The creature let out a final, pained roar as its arm shattered, the frozen rock breaking into pieces as it fell to the ground.

The Titan's body wavered one last time, and then, with a deafening crash, it finally toppled. Its massive form hit the ground with enough force to send shockwaves through the ice, the impact shattering the frozen surface beneath it.

For a moment, everything was still. The Titan lay motionless on the ground, its fiery form extinguished, its body now nothing more than a shattered, frozen husk. The soldiers hovered in the air above it, their weapons still trained on the creature, ready for any sign of movement.

But the Titan didn't move. It was finally down, its once-mighty form reduced to a pile of frozen rubble.

Grant let out a breath he'd been holding, his body relaxing as the adrenaline began to fade. He looked around at the soldiers hovering in the air around him, their faces a mix of exhaustion and relief.

"We did it," Plisetskaya said, her voice filled with awe as she looked down at the fallen Titan. "We actually did it."

"Yeah," Grant replied, his voice tired but triumphant. "We brought the damn thing down."

Harrows hovered beside them, his suit's thrusters humming softly as he surveyed the battlefield. "It's not over yet," he said, his voice calm but firm. "We need to secure the area and make sure there aren't any more surprises."

Grant nodded, his focus shifting from the fallen Titan to the task at hand. "Agreed. Let's get our teams on the ground and start sweeping the area. We need to make sure this thing is dead and that there aren't any more of them lurking around."

Plisetskaya nodded; her expression serious as she relayed the orders to her team. The soldiers began to descend, their suits guiding them to the ground as they prepared to secure the area.

As they landed on the ice, the soldiers moved with precision, their weapons at the ready as they began to sweep the area around the fallen Titan. The creature's body lay in a massive crater, the ice around it shattered and broken from the impact. The once-fiery form was now a cold, lifeless mass of rock, its molten core extinguished.

Harrows landed beside Grant and Plisetskaya, his eyes scanning the area for any signs of movement. "We need to be thorough," he said, his voice low. "We can't afford to leave anything to chance."

Grant nodded in agreement, his eyes narrowing as he looked down at the fallen Titan. "We'll make sure it's dead. And then we'll figure out what the hell to do next."

Plisetskaya nodded; her expression grim as she surveyed the battlefield. The fight was over but the war was far from won. The Titan was down but there were more out there, more threats that they would have to face.

But for now, they had won. The Titan was defeated, and the soldiers stood victorious on the icy battlefield, their breath fogging in the cold air as they prepared for whatever came next.

* * *

Back at Fort Blackwood, Marcus stared at the monitors, his cigarette forgotten between his fingers. The news of the Titan's destruction had just come in, and the control room buzzed with a mix of relief and exhaustion. He leaned back in his chair, eyes heavy with the weight of everything they had fought for, and everything they had lost.

"Well, that's one down," Marcus muttered to himself, but there was no satisfaction in his voice. His thoughts wandered to Nadia in Ukraine, to the horrors she must have witnessed, to the way their world had twisted into something unrecognizable. He had spent his life chasing the truth, but now that he had found it, he wished he hadn't. The price of knowledge, it seemed, was steep.

Harrows, who had just returned from the skyline, pulled off his helmet and took in a deep breath of the cold air. The rush of battle was fading, leaving behind a hollow silence that gnawed at him. He had seen too much and lost too many.

Jenkins.

His mind flashed back to the moment, the last-second effort to pull Jenkins out before everything exploded—the guilt weighed heavy on his chest. But there was no time to mourn. He looked around at what was left of his men, their faces gaunt, eyes haunted.

As the helicopter doors swung open, the Russian military medics began to disembark in case any of the survivors required immediate attention. Lieutenant Plisetskaya led the group, her presence commanding respect. She was an eye-catching figure in her white armor, her cropped hair and vitiligo giving her an almost unnatural appearance. When she approached Major Grant, there was an obvious acknowledgment of the battle they had just fought together, even if no words had been spoken of it. Grant, despite himself, was momentarily at a loss for words.

"Lieutenant," Grant said, finding his voice as he shook her hand. It was a brief, formal gesture, but at that moment, there was a spark of something more—something that neither of them had the luxury to explore.

Harrows, standing nearby, noticed the exchange and couldn't help but smirk. He had seen that look before, the one where a hardened soldier suddenly remembers there's more to life than just the fight. Rolling his eyes, Harrows let out a small, amused chuckle.

'Not now, Grant,' he thought to himself. But then again, in a world as shattered as theirs, who could blame him?

The Russian helicopters began to lift off, carrying Plisetskaya and her team back to their base. Grant watched them go, his thoughts briefly lingering on the Lieutenant before he forced himself to regain focus on the war. There was no time for distractions.

* * *

Back in the control room, the atmosphere was tense but not without a sense of accomplishment. The Titan's destruction was a victory, but no one was under any illusions—it was a small respite in a much larger crusade. Whitmore stood by the comms panel, exchanging formal acknowledgments and gratitude with the Russian command. There was a stiffness in the conversation, a tension that always underscored their mutual cooperation. Years of geopolitical, ideological and economic rivalries couldn't be wiped away in a single battle but for now, they were on the same side.

As the feed cut out, Whitmore glanced at Marcus, who was still petting Harrows' dog, Max, absentmindedly. Marcus gave a small nod, acknowledging the necessity of the alliance, no matter how uneasy it was. They had a long way to go, and the road ahead was uncertain.

The world had changed and would continue to change in ways none of them could have ever imagined. Breaches were still being reported, more monsters lurking in the shadows of their fractured reality, but they had proven that they could fight back. They had stood against the darkness and lived to tell the tale.

The reports of the Titan's destruction reached Dr. Shaw, who was going through some folders in her late mother's drawers. She allowed herself a moment of quiet reflection before humming and dialing Jeremiah's number to inform him as well.

There were still so many unknowns, so many variables that could tip the balance in favor of the darkness that loomed ever closer.

But for now, there was hope, and that was enough to keep them moving forward.

* * *

The Ukrainian bunker had withstood the tremors that had rocked the earth above. The quakes had been minor, but in the tense atmosphere of the bunker, they had felt like harbingers of Judgement. Now, however, the tremors had ceased, and the mood within the bunker shifted from dread to a cautious sense of peace.

News of the Titan's destruction had spread quickly, and though there was no celebration, a collective sigh of relief seemed to ripple through the bunker. Soldiers and scientists alike paused in their tasks, taking a moment to process the victory that had just been achieved. It was a small reprieve, a moment to catch their breath in the midst of a restless storm.

In the command center, the tension that had hung heavy in the air began to dissipate. Officers from Fort Blackwood had sent in a new list of commands and orders detailing the next steps in their fight against the breaches and the entities that had poured through them. The report spoke of the annihilation of Helena Voss and unknown whereabouts of Dr. Anton Weiss, who had been sucked into the vortex by one of the entities.

The officers explained that while the Titan had been vanquished, many breaches remained open worldwide, each a potential gateway for more horrors. The plan, they informed the bunker personnel, was to connect with other governments to form a global alliance, much like the temporary truce with the Russians that had proved successful. There was hope that a more permanent coalition could be formed to unite the world against the common threat.

Thomas Anderson, who had been pale and withdrawn throughout the ordeal, finally showed signs of life. His face, usually full of worry ever since the stationing, was now flushed with color as he absorbed the news. The joy he felt bubbled over, and he found himself babbling excitedly to Shade, who sat hunched beside in front of his screen, still as a statue.

"Can you believe it, Shade?" Thomas exclaimed, his voice full of awe. "We actually did it! We brought down a Titan! Everyone...everyone did their part, and you...you did an amazing job!"

Shade turned his eyes to look at Thomas, his expression unchanging, yet his eyes held a hint of something—bemusement, perhaps, or maybe a subtle embarrassment, though he had long abandoned basic decency to feel anything like that. For a moment, Shade seemed almost human.

Cho, who had been stretching out the kinks in his back, couldn't help but chuckle at the scene. He clapped Thomas on the shoulder, grinning at his enthusiasm.

"Don't get too carried away, Anderson," Cho teased. "He might bite you like a dog if you get too friendly."

Thomas blinked, clearly unprepared for a comment like that. "No, he-." He paused to meet Shade's piercing eyes once more and gulped. "Uh, maybe… I'll go talk to the tech guys real quick."

With that, the rangy young man backed away, moving to the other end of the room to speak to another fellow technician. Cho and Shade shared a look and Shade's lips curled in a way that the expression could almost pass for something close to a smile.

Meanwhile, in one of the labs, Nadia stood quietly, her eyes fixed on the containment capsule in front of her. She had come to observe Casca, the entity they had captured and immobilized. The creature was currently unconscious, its massive form doused in a chemical solution that kept it sedated and inert.

The lab was cold, the air humming with the low buzz of machinery. The more seasoned expert who had accompanied Nadia stood a few feet away, watching the monitors that displayed Casca's vital signs. He was here to ensure that everything was stable, that the creature remained contained and no longer posed a threat... and that Nadia didn't do something stupid like let it out. But Nadia's focus was elsewhere.

She just wanted to see Casca again. There was no scientific curiosity driving her, no need to gather more data or analyze the creature further. She simply wanted to look at him, to be in his presence. Despite everything that had happened, there was something about Casca that drew her in, something she couldn't quite explain.

Casca's massive form was sprawled within the capsule, its elongated, slender but muscular limbs held in place by restraints. Its skin, a mottled grey and black, was marred by the wounds it had sustained during its capture. No eyes, a horse-like black mane that ran down to the base of its neck, and a dog-like snout with jagged teeth inside. There was an undeniable visceral quality to it. And even in its current state, there was something majestic about the creature, something that hinted at a strength that had not been fully tapped.

Nadia's thoughts drifted as she stood there, memories of the last few days flashing through her mind. The fear, the uncertainty, the countless lives lost—all of it weighed on her as they did on all those involved. But there was also hope, a flash of light in the darkness that she clung to.

She continued to watch Casca, wondering what would come next. Her thoughts were interrupted by the sound of the door opening behind her. She turned to see the more seasoned expert stepping out, his task complete. He nodded to her as he left, leaving Nadia alone in the lab with Casca.

For a moment, she considered following him, returning to the command center where the rest of the team was gathered. But something kept her rooted to the spot, her eyes drawn back to the creature in the capsule.

She pondered if she had made the right decision by pleading to keep Casca alive. The other entities had been destroyed; their threat was deemed too great to allow them to continue existing in an enclosed underground area that was experiencing earthquakes. But Casca was different. It wasn't as unpredictable as the others, and there was a part of her that believed it could be trained and that it could be useful in the fight against the breaches.

Yet, naturally, the doubt lingered.

What if she was wrong?

What if keeping Casca alive was a mistake, one that would come back to haunt her? The responsibility weighed on her, but she couldn't bring herself to make the call.

Not yet.

With that, she finally turned away from Casca, her mind made up. She would speak with the others, discuss the options, and continue to defend the notion that Casca could prove to be a great ally. And for that, they needed to harden their resolve.

They needed to be smart and had to be careful.

As she left the lab, she glanced back at the capsule one last time. Casca remained unconscious, yet aware of all it could hear whenever anyone was close enough to his glass prison.

The bunker hummed with activity as preparations for the next phase of the operation began.

And something told her…it was going to be a while till she was with her parents again.

* * *

Zara Akhtar watched the frost slowly creep along the edges of her motel room window, its delicate patterns forming a lacework that hid the dreary world outside. The chill in the air seeped through the thin glass, but she hardly noticed it as she chewed on a piece of toast, her mind elsewhere. The news of the Titan's fall and Helena Voss's demise via Harrows had filled her with satisfaction. It wasn't a feeling of triumph, exactly—more of an appreciation that justice, in the best form, had been served.

Voss had been a menace, a symbol of everything wrong with the world and the Cabal's grip on it. The thought of Voss being crushed or incinerated brought a smile to Zara's lips. Harrows hadn't mentioned how she had died, though she could only hope it was painful. And Dr. Anton Weiss… the knowledge that he had escaped, pulled into that vortex by one of those entities, left a sour taste in her mouth. She prayed that whatever waited on the other side of that portal was as merciless as it seemed. Weiss deserved nothing less than to be torn apart, piece by piece, by the same horrors he had unleashed.

As Zara swallowed the dry toast, she thought of her mother, of Manchester. It had been less than a month, but it felt like a lifetime ago. The world had been different then, simpler in its own complicated way. Eesah, the mechanic she had met back home, found his way to her mind. If the world survived, if there was anything left worth holding on to, maybe she'd see if he was interested in marriage. The idea was old-fashioned, almost absurd, given everything that had happened. But the absurdity made her chuckle, a brief moment of levity in the midst of so much darkness.

The smile faded as quickly as it had come. She shook her head, thinking of Eesah and a future that might never come, feeling strangely out of place. The future was a nebulous thing, uncertain and fragile. But in moments like these, when the world reeled on the verge of downfall, those fleeting thoughts of what might have been were a small comfort.

With that, she stepped towards the bed and lay down. The frost continued to spread across the window, but Zara's mind was already sinking into the lure of sleep. The world outside was still as uncertain as ever. Tomorrow, or whenever she woke, there would be more battles to fight, more Cabal members to hunt down. But for now, she could rest, if only for a little while. She would allow herself the comfort of believing that humanity might just have a chance.

Even if it was a slim one.

Off in the world of dreams, she remained unaware of how the screen of her laptop lit up with an incoming text. One that would turn her mind upside down whenever she reads it.

"Bacha, it's me. I'm here."

Epilogue

Evelyn Shaw sat alone in the dim light of her office, the walls lined with books and the remnants of her latest forays into the unknown. The clock ticked past midnight, a gentle reminder of the world's relentless march forward. Her eyes, tired yet unyielding, scanned the open journal in front of her, filled with her neat, precise handwriting detailing the events that had unfolded.

As she closed the journal, her mind replayed the images of the breaches they had sealed and the faces of those they had lost. The weight of their sacrifices pressed heavily upon her, a constant companion in her quest for understanding and redemption. With a deep sigh, she leaned back in her chair, allowing herself a moment of quiet reflection.

The world had changed irrevocably. The breaches, though closed, had left scars in the fabric of reality that occasionally whispered secrets in the dead of night. Secrets that only those who had faced the void could truly understand. Evelyn knew that their work was far from done. The cabal, though scattered, still lurked in the shadows, their thirst for power unquenched.

Her thoughts were interrupted by the soft ping of her phone. It was a message from Marcus, containing only a cryptic note and an encrypted file. She opened it, her expert fingers quickly navigating the layers of security he had wrapped it in. The contents were disturbing—a report of minor but unusual energy fluctuations that matched none of their known patterns.

Evelyn felt the familiar stirrings of concern. They had hoped that closing the breaches would prevent further incursions, but the universe, it seemed, had other plans. She typed a quick response, agreeing to meet Marcus the next day. There was much to discuss, and the uneasy feeling in her gut told her that this was just the beginning.

As she prepared to leave, her gaze fell on a small, framed photograph on her desk. It was an old picture of her team, taken in a moment of triumph. Their smiles were wide, their spirits high. Now, looking at it, Evelyn felt a pang of sorrow for the simplicity of those days.

She turned off the light and stepped out of her office, the photograph still etched in her mind. The corridor was quiet; the only sound was the soft hum of the night shift's movements. As she walked, her resolve hardened. Whatever challenges lay ahead, she would face them head-on, armed with the knowledge and courage that had carried her this far.

Evelyn stepped out into the cool night air, the stars overhead shining brightly, silent witnesses to the dramas unfolding below. She looked up, feeling a connection to the cosmos that was both humbling and empowering. With a final deep breath, she started her car and drove into the night, ready to meet whatever awaited her with the dawn.

Evelyn drove through the sleeping city, her mind restless with the possibilities that Marcus's message hinted at. She knew too well that each anomaly could be a harbinger of deeper chaos, echoing the breaches they had fought so hard to close. The quiet streets seemed to mirror the calm before the storm, and Evelyn felt the weight of impending decisions heavy on her shoulders.

As she arrived at her modest home, the early hours of the morning cloaked everything in a deceptive peace. Inside, she headed straight to her study, a room filled with relics and research from their adventures, each object a token of their battles against the fabric of reality. She settled at her desk, surrounded by the gentle chaos of her work, and pulled out her notes on dimensional theory. Even now, the potential of what they had touched lingered at the edges of her understanding, promising and threatening in equal measure.

The next morning, Evelyn met Marcus at their usual café, a quiet spot that had become a haven for their discussions. Marcus was already there, his face etched with lines of concern that matched the urgency in his eyes.

"Thanks for coming, Evelyn," he greeted, pushing a cup of coffee toward her across the table.

Evelyn nodded, her expression serious as she opened her laptop and reviewed the data Marcus had sent. "These fluctuations," she started, her voice low, "they're not like anything we've seen before. They're subtle, but their pattern is... erratic. Almost as if they're probing, testing."

Marcus leaned in, his voice dropping to a whisper. "I've been tracking these anomalies for a few weeks now. They're spreading. Slowly, but spreading. And the places they appear... they're not random. They're strategic, near old breach sites and high-energy facilities."

The implications were clear, and a chill ran down Evelyn's spine. "The cabal," she murmured, "they're not just regrouping. They're advancing."

The conversation turned to the cabal, its remnants still woven into the fabric of the scientific and political elite. Despite their victory, the root of the cabal's influence remained entrenched, hidden within layers of secrecy and power. Evelyn and Marcus knew that to prevent another crisis, they would need to expose and dismantle these remnants completely.

"We need more allies," Evelyn stated, closing her laptop with a snap. "We need a network, eyes everywhere, ready to act before they can make another move."

Marcus nodded, his eyes hard with resolve. "I'll start reaching out to my contacts, see who can be trusted. We'll need people in science, government, media—everywhere."

In the days that followed, Evelyn took the first steps toward forming a new organization dedicated to monitoring dimensional science and its potential threats. With the support of a few trusted allies, they began to lay the groundwork for what would eventually become the Guardian Coalition, a group tasked with guarding against not just scientific abuses but also against any entities that might still lurk in the shadows of other dimensions.

As the Coalition gathered momentum, Evelyn found herself at the center of a new kind of battle; one fought in the shadows of bureaucracy and in the light of public scrutiny. Each day brought new challenges, but new allies were also drawn to the Coalition's cause.

Months later, at the inaugural conference of the Guardian Coalition, Evelyn stood before a crowd of the world's leading scientists, policymakers, and academics. Her speech was a blend of warning and hope, urging the world to learn from past mistakes and to move forward with caution and unity.

As she spoke, her words broadcasted worldwide, Evelyn knew that the road ahead would be fraught with challenges. But as she met the eyes of her team and her allies, she felt a surge of determination. They had closed the breaches once, and whatever came through next, they would be ready.